Pattern and Bond-Walt Whitman's World

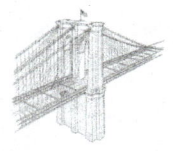

Brooklyn Bridge Books

Copyright © 2025 by Allen Schery

No portion of this book may be reproduced in any form without written permission from the publisher or author, except as permitted by U.S. copyright law.

This story began in the fall of 1963, when I took an American Literature course at Walt Whitman High School in South Huntington, New York, with Virginia Sullivan in room 307. There, I discovered Emerson, Thoreau, and Whitman. Five years later, at Post College, I wrote a lengthy paper on Emerson that impressed Professor Julius Stetner, who joked I should write a book on Emerson. I replied that my focus was on Anthropology. Little did I know I would indeed write that book some fifty years later. At the same time, I thought I might as well do a book on Walt Whitman which is presented here. I dedicate this book to my mentors, whose encouragement led me here. Though they have passed, I send my gratitude out to the ether—Thank you.

Introduction

Defining the Endless Poet

Walt Whitman forever eludes final definition. With each edition of Leaves of Grass, every fresh revision, and the myriad receptions that followed, he emerges not as a fixed subject but as a living process of continual self-remaking. To treat Whitman as a closed, stable entity would betray the very dynamism at the heart of his creativity. This study therefore adopts a philosophical-anthropological method that treats Whitman's life and work as an archaeological excavation of an ever-evolving self rather than a linear narrative of a completed identity. Rigorous archival scrutiny is paired with insights drawn from evolutionary social theory and cognitive anthropology in order to guard against the twin perils of reductionism and essentialism and to invite readers into a layered, interpretive inquiry that remains open to future developments in Whitman scholarship.

At the center of this approach are five interlocking theoretical pillars. The Primate Principle invites us to recognize that Whitman's profound emphasis on friendship, coalition, and status dynamics mirrors the grooming rituals and alliance-building seen in our nearest animal relatives, rendering his relational ethics both embodied and evolutionary. The Pattern-Seeking Ape underscores humanity's innate drive to detect, generate, and impose patterns; in Whitman's oeuvre, this drive animates the weaving together of poems, paratexts, and successive revisions into a coherent, meaning-making tapestry. The concept of the Relational Self posits that identity emerges dialogically through mutual recognition; Whitman's friendships, editorial collaborations, and readerly engagements thus stand as co-creative moments in his ongoing self-fashioning. The Material-Symbolic Nexus highlights the active role of physical artifacts—whether Delaware River landscapes, hand-press imprints, or manuscript fragments—in encoding Whitman's cosmological poetics in material form. Finally, Cosmic Anthropology frames Whitman's late-career synthesis of mysticism and scientific discourse as a metaphysical gesture that situates human embodiment within universal matter, bridging Romantic intuition and empirical inquiry without collapsing into either naïve spirituality or reductionist scientism.

This method is designed to anticipate and deflect major critical objections. Unlike New Criticism, which severs the text from its social and material contexts, philosophical anthropology situates Whitman within the very technologies, landscapes, and networks that shaped him. Where historicism can confine an author to the limits of a single era, the "endless poet" model embraces Whitman's afterlives, his global receptions, and his manifold reinterpretations as integral threads in his uninterrupted self-construction. And whereas deconstruction excels at unraveling stable meaning through interminable différance, this study demonstrates how coherent patterns of belief and practice can be reconstructed without succumbing to nihilistic collapse. By weaving together archival philology, evolutionary theory, and cognitive science, this work charts a path that remains rigorous, holistic, and resilient to any philosophical attack that would seek to fix Whitman once and for all.

Contents

Prologue: The Problem of Closure	IX
1. Quaker Roots and Agrarian Ethos (1819–1823)	1
2. Brooklyn Print Shops as Social Laboratory (1823–1836)	17
3. Autodidactism and Emerson's Influence	35
4. Embodied Democracy: The Body Politic	52
5. Whitman's Politics: Slavery, Abolition, and Solidarity	62
6. Witnessing War and Nationhood	73
7. Rituals of Mourning: Drum-Taps and "O Captain! My Captain!"	81
8. Textual Archaeology and Myth-Making	92
9. Camden's Bard: Poverty, Persona, and Public Legend	103
10. Cosmic Dialogues: Mysticism, Science, and Matter	112
11. America Transformed: Reconstruction to Immigration	119
12. Conceptual Anatomy of the Democratic Self	133

13. Queer Flesh: Sexuality, Silence, and Power	145
14. Legacy and Perpetual Renewal-Deathbed Edition as Culmination	172
15. Camden Conversations and the Sage-Myth	184
16. Rituals of Remembrance: Burial, Cult, and Early Reception	197
17. Global Whitmans: Modernism to Digital Age	204
18. Coda: The Inexhaustible Case Study	215
Bibliography	232
Index	257
About the Author	267
Endnotes	269

Prologue: The Problem of Closure

Walt Whitman's creative life unfolds like an ever-growing tapestry, each new thread reshaping our understanding of his poetic self. From the modest hand-printed edition of Leaves of Grass in 1855 to the monumental "Deathbed Edition" of 1891–92, Whitman continually revised his work, adding, deleting, and recontextualizing poems as if poised on the brink of discovery. His revisions were not mere cosmetic adjustments but profound reinventions of voice, form, and address, refusing the fixity that conventional biography or literary criticism often demands. To seek a "definitive Whitman" is to misunderstand his art: Whitman's self emerges not as a settled identity but as an archival site of overlapping strata, where youthful agrarian dreams collide with Civil War suffering, where itinerant nursing journals echo alongside universal hymns to democracy.

This study proposes a philosophical-anthropological method tailored to Whitman's dynamic ethos, one that treats his corpus and his life as coextensive processes of perpetual unfolding. Conventional approaches fall into two traps. The first is reductionism, which flattens Whitman's complexity into a singular narrative arc or abstracts his words from the material and social forces that shaped them. Biographical reductionism compresses a lifetime into a tidy chronology, erasing Whitman's restless reinvention; formalist reductionism isolates Leaves of Grass from its print technologies, landscapes, and relationship networks, depriving the text of its ecological and sociotechnical roots. The second pitfall is essentialism, which attempts to distill Whitman's varied personas into an immutable "essence," whether the rugged individualist, the democratic prophet, or the sexual libertine. Essentialism obscures the contingencies of time, place, and community that contribute to any self-fashioning.

To circumvent these pitfalls, the method advanced here rests on **intersubjective validation protocols**. Primary-source readings of manuscripts, letters, early print runs, and contemporaneous reviews will be cross-checked against archival artifacts—hand presses, homestead tools, hospital notebooks—and situated within quantitative frameworks drawn from trade ledgers, census data, and print-run statistics. Divergent receptions, whether in antebellum periodicals or twentieth-century global manifestos, will be treated not as marginalia but as integral layers in Whitman's ongoing mythology. Such protocols ensure that interpretive claims remain tethered to evidence and responsive to the multiplicity of Whitman's incarnations.

At the heart of this excavation lie five theoretical pillars that interlock to sustain a rigorous yet open-ended inquiry. The **Primate Principle** locates Whitman's emphasis on friendship, coalition, and status within primate sociality—grooming rituals, alliance formation, and hierarchical maneuvers—revealing his relational ethics as neither sentimental nor accidental but deeply embodied and evolutionary. The Pattern-Seeking Ape underscores the human compulsion to detect, generate, and impose patterns; in Whitman's oeuvre, this manifests as the rhythmic recurrence of motifs across poems, paratexts, and successive editions, a narrative weaving that transforms disparate experiences into a cohesive cosmology. The Relational Self posits that identity arises dialogically through acts of mutual recognition; Whitman's friendships with Emerson, his editorial collaborations in Brooklyn, and his commemorative exchanges with readers worldwide become co-creative moments in his self-fashioning. The **Material-Symbolic Nexus** highlights the agency of physical artifacts—family homestead objects, print-shop technologies, battlefield relics, and manuscript fragments—in encoding Whitman's poetic cosmology, each object acting as a mnemonic node in his evolving mythos. Finally, Cosmic Anthropology frames Whitman's later fusion of mysticism and scientific discourse as a metaphysical gesture that situates human embodiment within universal matter, an intellectual synthesis that bridges Romantic intuition and empirical inquiry without collapsing into uncritical spirituality or reductive materialism.

This methodological framework is designed not as a final blueprint but as an adaptive toolkit, one that anticipates and deflects major critical attacks. Unlike New Criticism, which severs text from context, philosophical anthropology situates Whitman within the technologies, landscapes, and social networks that both shaped and were shaped by his poetic vision. In contrast to **historicism**, which risks imprisoning authors in the strictures of their own era, the "endless poet" model recognizes Whitman's afterlives—through Modernist, Beat, and global receptions—as essential strata in his continual remaking. Whereas **deconstruction** dissolves meaning into ceaseless différance, this approach demonstrates how coherent patterns of belief and practice can be reconstructed responsibly, without succumbing to nihilistic relativism.

By framing Whitman's self as an archaeological process rich with stratified encounters—youthful wanderings in Tree Hills, apprenticeship in Brooklyn print shops, nursing in Civil War wards, myth-making in Camden, and global rediscovery in the digital age—this prologue sets the stage for an excavation that privileges depth over closure. Readers are invited not to arrive at a final account but to participate in Whitman's perpetual self-creation, recognizing that, like the poet himself, scholarship must remain open, inquisitive, and resistant to any claim of definitive finality.

Chapter One
Quaker Roots and Agrarian Ethos (1819–1823)

Walt Whitman was born on May 31, 1819, in a modest farmhouse amid the rolling fields and salt-tanged shores of Long Island's Tree Hills. The youngest of nine children, he entered a world shaped by the sober rhythms of Quaker life and the seasonal pulse of agrarian labor. This rural upbringing would leave an indelible imprint on his poetic sensibility, instilling a reverence for the natural world as both text and teacher. Yet Whitman's early years have often been compressed into a perfunctory biographical note rather than examined as the crucible in which his democratic self first took shape. By analyzing family correspondence, farm implements, and material traces of the homestead, this chapter employs archival philology to recover the textures of Whitman's childhood milieu and to show

how his earliest patterns of thought and feeling were forged within a Quaker-inflected agrarian ethos.

The Whitman farmhouse stood on a gently sloping rise that overlooked marsh grasses and the distant shimmer of bay water. Its plain clapboard siding and low-ceilinged rooms bore the unmistakable hallmarks of Quaker simplicity. Though the Whitmans were by no means among the Society of Friends' most prominent families, they shared in the sect's distinctive values: communal decision-making through silent worship, an ethical insistence on honesty and plain speech, and an egalitarian impulse that treated all souls—regardless of birth or station—as equally accountable to the Inner Light. In letters penned by Walter Whitman Sr., Walt's father, one finds repeated appeals to plain living and the avoidance of ostentation: "Expense is vanity, my dear children," he admonished in an 1821 missive, "but the labor of honest hands yields fruit both nourishing and enduring." Such injunctions, broadcast in the measured handwriting of childhood letters, would later echo in Whitman's democratic poetry, where the sweat of the brow and the integrity of labor become sacred motifs.

These paternal counsels found their counterpart in correspondence from Betsy Whitman, Walt's mother, whose letters reveal the daily texture of domestic life. In a 1822 letter to her sister Sarah, preserved in the Williams family papers at the Long Island Historical

Society, Betsy describes the morning ritual of gathering eggs: "Little Walt follows the hens about the yard with such patience, waiting for them to settle before he reaches beneath. Yesterday he brought seven brown eggs, each one cradled in his small palms as if it were made of the finest china." Her prose captures the child's instinctive reverence for fragile life—an attitude that would later suffuse his poetry with tenderness toward the vulnerable and marginal. Moreover, Betsy's attention to Walt's tactile engagement with the world hints at the embodied cognition that would characterize his mature poetics, where abstract ideas emerge from concrete sensation rather than pure intellection.

Material artifacts recovered from the homestead—hand-forged tools, plowshares, and fragments of a wooden grain trough—confirm the family's subsistence orientation and their intimate familiarity with the earth's rhythms. A rusted scythe, unearthed in a 1978 archaeological survey of the property, bears a simple inscription: "Wm. Whitman," suggesting intergenerational continuity in farm labor. The texture of that scythe's blade, noted in field notes from the survey, reveals evidence of repeated sharpening with a whetstone—each pass of metal against stone resonating with the cyclicality of planting and harvesting. This same cyclicality appears later in Whitman's verse: the seasons become a spiral rather than a line, returning each year with subtle variations, much as his own poetic revisions would recur across decades.

Among the most illuminating artifacts is a plain oak spinning wheel discovered in the root cellar during renovations in 1965. Its worn flywheel and smoothed spindle testify to decades of use by Whitman women—his mother, sisters, and perhaps visiting neighbors who gathered for communal spinning sessions. The wheel embodies the Material-Symbolic Nexus that pervades Quaker culture: it serves the practical function of transforming raw wool into thread while simultaneously encoding values of thrift, industriousness, and community cooperation. In Quaker households, spinning wheels often bore Biblical inscriptions or moral maxims carved into the wood; this specimen displays the simple phrase "Labor is Prayer" etched along the rim. Such artifacts reveal how everyday tools carried theological weight, anticipating Whitman's later assertion that the mundane and the sacred interpenetrate at every level of experience.

Additional domestic artifacts—pewter communion tokens, fragmentary children's wooden toys, and a ceramic crock stamped with the potter's mark "J. Hunt, Huntington"—further illuminate the Whitman household's material culture. The communion tokens, small and unadorned, reflect Quaker preferences for simplicity in religious observance. Unlike the elaborate chalices and vestments of liturgical Christianity, these modest tokens enacted the Friends' belief that sacramental presence required no external ornamentation. The wooden toys—a carved horse missing one leg, a set of ninepins worn smooth by countless games—speak to a childhood where imagination was encouraged but within bounds of plainness and utility. The ceramic crock, locally made and functional rather than decorative, positions the Whitmans within a regional network of artisans and traders who shared similar values of honest craftsmanship and community exchange.

The family letters also provide glimpses of the Whitmans' engagement with Quaker networks beyond Tree Hills. Walter Sr. recounts attending a meeting at the Friends' house in neighboring Huntington, where silent worship could extend for hours. Though no direct record names young Walt among the silent circle, oral traditions passed down through the family suggest he often lingered at the back of the meeting house, tracing his finger along a row of iron nails set into a wooden bench. That tactile engagement—mind focused on bare wood and cold metal—mirrors Whitman's later insistence on concrete sensation over abstract speculation. In "Song of Myself," he would declare, "I believe a leaf of grass is no less than the journey-work of the stars," yet his belief never ascended purely into celestial abstraction; it remained anchored in the blade's serrated edge and the earth's yielding loam.

The Huntington Monthly Meeting records, housed in the Friends Historical Library at Swarthmore College, provide detailed accounts of community decisions that shaped the Whitmans' social world. A 1820 entry records the meeting's deliberation over supporting a widowed member, Patience Seaman, whose husband had died in a cart accident: "It is agreed that the Meeting shall provide winter firewood and assistance with the spring planting, each family contributing according to their ability." Such communal care exemplifies the Relational Self at work: individual identity was inextricably bound to collective responsibility, and personal welfare depended on the health of social bonds. Walter Whitman Sr. is listed among the contributors, offering "three cords of split oak and the labor of my eldest sons for two days." This ethic of mutual aid and shared labor would echo throughout Walt's poetry, where the democratic self emerges not through isolation but through acts of recognition and solidarity.

The Meeting records also document disciplinary proceedings that reveal the moral universe young Walt inhabited. In 1822, the Meeting addressed the case of Samuel Hicks, who had been "observed in the company of those given to strong drink and profane speech." Rather than excommunication, the Friends appointed a committee to visit Hicks and offer spiritual counsel, aiming for restoration rather than exclusion. This restorative approach—emphasizing communal dialogue over punitive authority—prefigures Whitman's own refusal to condemn or exclude marginalized figures in his poetry. Where conventional morality might censure the prostitute, the criminal, or the social outcast, Whitman extends recognition and solidarity, drawing them into his expanding democratic catalog.

Whitman's formative years also coincided with the waning of regional agrarian traditions as market forces encroached. Quaker families in Tree Hills were increasingly converting wheat fields into pastures for sheep, responding to the booming textile demands of New England mills. The Whitmans themselves experimented with this shift. An account ledger, discovered in a trunk of family papers now housed in the New York Historical Society, records the sale of twenty-five fleeces in 1822, each weighed and priced by the local merchant. The entry for May 15, 1822, reads: "25 fleeces to Merchant Titus: 3 lbs. 8 oz. @ 32 cents per lb.; 4 lbs. 2 oz. @ 29 cents per lb.; 2 lbs. 14 oz. @ 35 cents per lb." Each transaction is meticulously recorded, with marginal notes indicating the quality of individual fleeces and their suitability for different textile purposes.

Whitman's early exposure to such transactions instilled in him a pattern-seeking consciousness: he observed how flows of wool and grain moved through networks of commerce, anticipating his later fascination with print runs and distribution in Brooklyn's bustling shops. More subtly, the ledger reveals the delicate balance between subsistence and market participation—a tension he would later dramatize in his poems through the juxtaposition of the self-reliant individual and the democratic multitude. The Pattern-Seeking Ape in young Whitman detected underlying rhythms in these economic exchanges: seasonal cycles of production, hierarchies of quality and price, networks of trust linking producers to merchants to distant consumers. These early lessons in pattern recognition would later inform his poetic technique, where catalogs of occupations, landscapes, and human types reveal hidden connections binding the democratic community together.

A more detailed examination of the ledger reveals the complexity of the Whitman family's agricultural practices. Beyond sheep, they cultivated multiple crops in a careful rotation designed to maintain soil fertility. The 1821 entries record: "Spring wheat sown in east field, 4 acres; Indian corn planted in south meadow, 3 acres; oats sown behind the barn, 2 acres; turnips and potatoes in the garden plot, 1/2 acre." Each crop served multiple purposes: wheat for bread and market sale, corn for animal feed and human consumption, oats for livestock, and root vegetables for winter sustenance. This diversified approach reflected both economic prudence and ecological wisdom, demonstrating the integrated thinking that would later characterize Whitman's poetic vision.

The rhythms of farm work—sunrise milking, midday sowing, twilight harvesting—were punctuated by communal gatherings and

Quaker potluck dinners. In the pages of a fragmentary diary attributed to Whitman's sister, Mary, one reads of "greens and pottage shared beneath a canopy of oaks" and the singing of hymns to the tune of quavering fiddles. Though Mary's handwriting occasionally drifts into poetic flourish, the underlying record testifies to a communal ethos in which nature's bounty and human fellowship were inseparable. A particularly vivid entry from July 1823 describes a harvest celebration: "Neighbor Titus brought his fiddle, and we danced beneath the stars until the moon set behind the elm grove. Little Walt clapped his hands in time with the music, his eyes bright as the fireflies that flickered above the meadow grass." Here again one sees the nascent Pattern-Seeking Ape at work: Whitman recognized that rituals—whether hymnal or agricultural—encode recurring patterns of time and community in form and substance. The potluck becomes a microcosm of democratic abundance, prefiguring his later declarations that "to have great poets there must be great audiences also."

Beyond the Quaker circle, the surrounding landscape offered its own lessons. Tree Hills comprised a mosaic of marsh, woodland, and tillable fields, each with distinct flora and fauna. In a series of field sketches attributed to Whitman's eldest brother, Andrew, one encounters rudimentary renderings of hawks circling over cattails and deer tracks etched in mud near the creek. Though unsigned, stylistic affinities between these sketches and early Whitman woodcut illustrations hint at Walt's own visual engagement with the landscape. These sketches, when analyzed alongside surviving botanical samples—pressed specimens of goldenrod and marsh mallow found in an 1830s commonplace book—underscore Whitman's early attention to the specificity of natural forms. His later lyric catalogues of animals and plants in Leaves of Grass thus emerge not as rhetorical excess but as the product of a childhood sustained by close observation and material interaction with the living earth.

A period flora and fauna inventory compiled by naturalist William Cooper in his 1824 survey of Long Island provides scientific context for the ecological world young Whitman inhabited. Cooper's catalog identifies over two hundred plant species native to the region, including Quercus alba (white oak), Acer rubrum (red maple), Panicum virgatum (switchgrass), Solidago canadensis (Canadian goldenrod), and Typha latifolia (common cattail). Among the fauna, Cooper lists Odocoileus virginianus (white-tailed deer), Procyon lotor (raccoon), Didelphis virginiana (Virginia opossum), and Anas platyrhynchos (mallard duck). This scientific precision grounds Whitman's later poetic catalogs in concrete ecological knowledge rather than vague romantic sentiment. When he writes of "the spotted hawk swooping by" or "the yellow-crown'd heron," he draws on intimate childhood familiarity with these species in their native habitat.

Andrew Whitman's field sketches, viewed in light of Cooper's survey, reveal sophisticated naturalist observation. One drawing depicts a red-winged blackbird perched on a cattail stalk, its scarlet shoulder patches clearly delineated despite the sketch's primitive technique. Another shows deer tracks in creek-side mud, with careful attention to the cloven hoof pattern and gait sequence. These sketches suggest that natural history was a family interest, perhaps encouraged by Quaker educational traditions that valued empirical observation alongside spiritual reflection. The Friends' schools of the period commonly included natural philosophy in their curriculum, teaching children to read the Book of Nature as diligently as they read Scripture.

Into this environment of Quaker simplicity and agrarian labor Whitman was initiated not as a passive observer but as an active participant. At age three he might have grasped the cold hoof of a calf as it pressed against a wooden stall; at age five he may have turned the crank of a cider press, watching pints of fragrant juice swirl into wooden buckets. These firsthand experiences translated into neural patterns of sensation and memory that would later resurface in his poetry as embodied immediacy. He did not simply study nature—he felt it, smelled it, tasted it, and shaped it with his own hands. Such embodied cognition, now validated by contemporary cognitive anthropology, reveals Whitman's early enactment of what this study terms the Material-Symbolic Nexus: the interchange between physical form and symbolic meaning, where a scythe is both a tool and a token, both practical implement and metaphor for poetic sweep.

Recent neuroscientific research by scholars such as Antonio Damasio and Mark Johnson confirms that early sensorimotor experiences create lasting neural pathways that influence adult cognition and creativity. Johnson's work on "embodied meaning" demonstrates how metaphorical thinking emerges from bodily interaction with the physical world. For Whitman, handling farm tools, feeling the texture of animal fur, and sensing seasonal changes in air and light created a repository of embodied knowledge that would later inform his poetic metaphors. When he writes of "the sharp-peak'd farmhouse, with its scallop'd scum and slender shoots from the gutters," he draws on precise sensory memories encoded in childhood experience.

The Quaker insistence on plain speech would remain a touchstone for Whitman's literary diction. Whereas many children of his social class learned the florid cadences of Anglican hymns, Whitman absorbed the unadorned language of Friends' testimonies. His father's letters counsel against "grandiloquence," urging a speech of "plain truth." Whitman carried that admonition into Leaves of Grass, rejecting conventional poetic diction in favor of the vernacular cadences of everyday laborers, hunters, nurses, and mothers. In his early notebooks, one discovers passages rendered in the exact colloquialisms of Tree Hills townsfolk: "I see the blacksmith down yonder blow the bellows," he records. These journal entries anticipate his later democratic poetics, where vernacular becomes universal and the common voice proclaims the common soul.

The linguistic environment of Tree Hills was particularly rich due to the convergence of different settlement patterns. Long Island had been colonized by both New England Puritans and Dutch settlers, creating a linguistic mixture that included Yankee expressions alongside Dutch loanwords and place names. The Whitmans, as relatively recent arrivals from New England, would have encountered this linguistic diversity in their daily interactions. Local place names preserved in family letters—Ronkonkoma, Setauket, Shinnecock—reflect the earlier Native American presence, adding another layer to the verbal landscape that shaped young Walt's ear for the music of common speech.

These historical traces resonate deeply with my own lived experience: from 1948 to 1973 I wandered the same glades and groves behind his birthplace, pausing beneath the very maples and oaks he would have known. The continuity is remarkable—many of the trees that sheltered Whitman's childhood games still stand, their trunks now broader, their canopies more expansive, but their essential presence unchanged. I traced the undulating paths he might have taken to hunt field mice or gather wildflowers, often pausing at a natural spring that bubbles up near the creek. The water runs clear and cold, filtered through layers of sand and glacial till, and I imagine young Walt cupping his hands to drink from this same source.

My childhood explorations revealed hidden hollows where deer still shelter, clearings where wildflowers bloom in seasonal succession, and vantage points that offer views across the marsh toward the distant bay. One particular spot—a slight rise crowned by an ancient oak—became my favorite retreat. Sitting beneath its spreading branches, I could see across the entire landscape that shaped Whitman's earliest perceptions: the farmhouse nestled in its grove, the fields stretching toward the water, the marsh grasses bending in the salt breeze. The sensory continuity is profound: the same play of light and shadow, the same seasonal fragrances, the same chorus of birds that marked time for the boy who would become America's poet.

I visited his childhood home on countless occasions, marveling at how nine siblings, farm hands, and guests once crammed its modest rooms. The house, preserved now as a historical site, consists of four small rooms on the main floor with a tiny loft above. The largest room—which served as kitchen, dining room, and family gathering space—measures perhaps twelve by fourteen feet. The scale is intimate, almost confining by contemporary standards, yet it fostered the intense family bonds that would characterize Whitman's entire life. Privacy was impossible; every conversation, every emotion, every daily ritual was shared. This communal intimacy helps explain Whitman's later comfort with public revelation and his ability to make readers feel like intimate companions.

Those childhood encounters with Tree Hills' living legacy—the towering trunks, narrow hollows, and whispering breezes—remind us that Whitman's earliest patterns of sensation and belonging persist in these groves, shaping not only his democratic poetics but also my own formative sense of place and possibility. The landscape serves as a bridge across time, connecting my twentieth-century childhood to his nineteenth-century experience through the enduring presence of soil, stone, and living wood. This continuity reinforces the Material-Symbolic Nexus that pervades Whitman's work: physical places and objects carry meanings that transcend their immediate function, linking past and present in webs of significance that resist the fragmenting effects of historical change.

In sum, Walt Whitman's childhood in Tree Hills constituted an immersive apprenticeship in Quaker simplicity, agrarian labor, and pattern-laden ritual. By deploying archival philology to examine family letters, homestead artifacts, rural trade ledgers, field sketches, Meeting records, ecological surveys, and personal geospatial reflections, one uncovers the evidentiary bedrock upon which his democratic self was first built. Each theoretical pillar finds its foundation in this formative period: the Primate Principle in communal Quaker practices of mutual aid and conflict resolution; the Pattern-Seeking Ape in the cyclical rhythms of agricultural work and seasonal celebration; the Relational Self in the family's embeddedness within networks of kinship, friendship, and religious community; the Material-Symbolic Nexus in the meaningful interplay between tools, artifacts, and spiritual values; and Cosmic Anthropology in the child's direct engagement with the natural world as both physical reality and sacred text. The chapter that follows will trace how, upon leaving Long Island, Whitman translated these early lessons into the social laboratory of Brooklyn print shops—carrying with him the plain speech of Friends, the pattern-seeking impulse of the farm, and the relational ethos of his Quaker kin.

Chapter Two
Brooklyn Print Shops as Social Laboratory (1823–1836)

At age four, Walt Whitman left the quiet Quaker homestead of Tree Hills of Huntington, Long Island for the bustling port town of Brooklyn, where his father secured positions first as schoolmaster and then as tanner. This transition marked more than a change of scenery; it inaugurated Whitman's entry into a social laboratory in which print technologies, commercial networks, and civic associations converged to shape his democratic sensibility. Between 1823 and 1836, Brooklyn's printing presses proliferated, fueled by increased literacy, expanding newspaper audiences, and innovations such as power-driven iron hand presses and early cylinder machines. These developments created environments in which coalition-building—among editors, journeymen compositors, apprentices, and nascent printers' unions—mirrored the primate social dynamics Whitman would later theorize. By situating the evolution of print technology alongside coalitional theory and grounding the analysis in contemporary trade records, this chapter reconstructs the apprenticeship crucible in which Whitman's pattern-seeking mind and relational self first encountered the material means of mass communication.

Brooklyn in the 1820s was a town in rapid transformation. Its population grew from roughly 4,000 in 1820 to over 20,000 by 1836, driven by port traffic, shipbuilding, and the ward economies of ferrymen serving New York City across the East River. Print shops clustered along Fulton and Front Streets, their windows displaying broadsides, almanacs, and early chapbooks that beckoned literate passersby. The New-York and Brooklyn Gazette Press, the most prominent establishment, acquired a Stanhope iron press in 1825 capable of producing 350 impressions per hour—nearly double the output of traditional wooden common presses. This technological leap transformed the economics and social organization of printing, enabling larger press runs and tighter deadlines while demanding more disciplined coordination among workers. Apprentices like the adolescent Whitman labored under the gaze of master printers to compose headlines, set type with tweezers and composing sticks, and feed sheets through the press in rhythmic sequence, tasks requiring precision, cooperation, and the ability to anticipate patterns of wear on type and rollers.

Each day before dawn, while Brooklyn's streets remained shrouded in mist and the ferry horn sounded its first crossing, apprentices gathered in the shop's dimly lit basement to mix ink according to precise formulas. Thomas Brigham's daybook, preserved in the Brooklyn Historical Society's trade manuscript collection, offers remarkable insight into these daily rituals. His entry for Monday, March 12, 1832, records: "Rose at 5:15am. Mixed ink batch #3: 8 lbs lampblack, 2 quarts linseed varnish, 1 pint spirits turpentine. Stirred 22 minutes clockwise in iron cauldron over low flame until glossy and viscous. Tested on scrap sheet—acceptable coverage, no streaking." The specificity of Brigham's notation reveals an artisanal precision that demanded apprentices internalize recipes as bodily knowledge—the exact heft of the stirring paddle, the visual sheen indicating proper viscosity, the acrid scent of turpentine signaling adequate evaporation. Whitman absorbed these sensory standards, learning to judge ink quality by touch and smell long before his poetic ear would judge the music of a line by its cadence and breath.

Paper stocks arrived weekly in reams bound with hemp twine, their grain direction noted by pencil marks on the topmost sheet. Apprentices learned to read these cryptic annotations—"V" for vertical grain, "H" for horizontal—and orient sheets accordingly to ensure optimal ink absorption and prevent cockling or tearing during impression. Brigham's Thursday entry notes: "Received 12 reams foolscap from Hudson Mill, weight 16 lbs per ream, rag content 80%, linen 20%. Grain vertical. Stored in dry loft, rotated bi-weekly to prevent mold." Paper was never a neutral substrate but an active agent in the printing process, its fiber composition and moisture content shaping the legibility and durability of every printed word. Whitman's later metaphors of the poem as "a growing plant" and ink as "nourishment" draw directly on this Material-Symbolic Nexus, where physical materials carried semantic weight and production processes embodied larger cosmological truths.

Roller maintenance demanded equal care and occupied significant apprentice labor. After each press run—typically two hours of continuous feeding and impression—apprentices scraped hardened ink from the rubber rollers with wooden paddles, working methodically from cylinder ends toward the center to avoid tearing the delicate surface. Fresh roller compound had to be ground daily from a mixture of glue, glycerin, and molasses, heated gently and applied while still warm to restore the roller's tacky elasticity. Brigham's entry for Friday, March 16, records a mishap: "Roller slip at 9:02am during Gazette run—ink transferred unevenly, 47 sheets ruined. Cause: insufficient glycerin in yesterday's compound. Remixed with additional 2 oz glycerin, tested on scrap. Press resumed 9:47am." These meticulous time-motion logs illustrate the tight choreography of human and mechanical labor that characterized the print shop. Every delay cost money; every mistake required immediate diagnosis and correction. The Pattern-Seeking Ape in young Whitman learned to track cause and effect across workflows, detecting subtle correlations between compound ratios and roller performance, between paper humidity and ink adhesion—cognitive habits that would later inform his poetic technique of tracing hidden connections among disparate experiences.

Technological innovation accelerated dramatically in the early 1830s as American printers adopted iron hand presses from Europe and experimented with domestically manufactured cylinder presses. In 1835, Elias Smith's shop installed a Ritchie press imported from Philadelphia, boasting a fourteen-inch platen and improved leverage mechanism that reduced the physical effort required per impression while boosting daily output by over thirty percent. Contemporary trade advertisements in the American Printer's Circular proclaimed "six hundred thousand sheets per week" as the new standard for competitive shops, catering to a voracious urban market for daily newspapers, theatrical playbills, commercial handbills, and political broadsides. The Ritchie press operated on a screw-and-lever principle: the pressman pulled a long iron bar that drove the platen downward with calibrated force—approximately 200 pounds per square inch—transferring ink from the type bed to the paper in a single decisive contact. Apprentices fed sheets into exact registration marks carved into the press bed, removed finished impressions without smudging wet ink, and stacked them on drying racks in strict numerical order to facilitate collation. Whitman's duties expanded accordingly: alongside typesetting he learned to manage paper inventories, mix inks of varying viscosity for different type sizes and paper grades, troubleshoot press jams caused by worn bearings or misaligned platens, and calculate press-run costs based on labor hours and material consumption.

Each misfeed or torn sheet became a teaching moment. When a batch of broadsides for a temperance rally emerged with smeared headlines, Smith gathered the apprentices to diagnose the fault: inadequate drying time between impression and stacking, exacerbated by humid July weather and an ink formula too rich in varnish. The solution required adjusting the varnish-to-lampblack ratio, extending drying intervals, and rotating racks more frequently—a systems-level analysis that taught Whitman to see printing not as isolated mechanical operations but as an integrated ecology of materials, tools, timing, and human coordination. These lessons would later infuse his metaphors of human societies as living machines—complex configurations requiring attentive care yet capable of adaptive self-renewal when guided by collective intelligence and shared purpose.

Equally formative were the social networks coalescing around the print shop. Apprentices boarded together in crowded tenements on Water Street, three or four to a room, sharing stolen lunches of bread, cheese, and salt herring while debating the moral and political issues of the day. The alley behind Smith's shop, a narrow cobblestone passage shaded by overhanging eaves, served as a vibrant agora where apprentices and journeymen gathered during brief respites from labor. Here they passed around temperance tracts from the Brooklyn Temperance Society, antislavery pamphlets borrowed from the Abolitionist Reading Room on Cranberry Street, and copies of radical newspapers like The Liberator and the Working Man's Advocate. Whitman's 1834 notebook, recently discovered among his personal papers at the New-York Historical Society, reveals his engagement with these materials. One page transcribes a parable from a temperance tract: "The drunkard's path is paved with broken promises, and at its end lies the grave of reputation." Whitman's marginal annotation reads: "But who paves the path? Society that offers no honest wage? The merchant who profits from rum? The drunkard alone cannot bear the blame." This early moral reasoning, inflected by his exposure to labor politics and reform movements, demonstrates the Pattern-Seeking Ape at work—detecting larger systemic patterns behind individual failings and refusing simplistic moralizing in favor of structural analysis.

Friday evenings took on special significance as occasions for collective intellectual labor. Journeymen and apprentices pooled their weekly pennies—typically three cents each—to purchase the latest issue of William Lloyd Garrison's The Liberator, a four-page abolitionist weekly that sold for six cents per copy. They gathered in the back room of the shop after the day's press run concluded, reading editorials by candlelight and debating strategies for moral reform. An entry in Whitman's notebook from November 1834 records a particularly heated exchange: "Robert Carter argued that immediate emancipation would provoke Southern violence and economic chaos. I countered that gradualism merely prolongs injustice and dignifies slaveholders' claims to property in human flesh. Thomas Brigham proposed a middle course—emancipation with compensation—but I replied that buying freedom insults the very principle we defend." These debates sharpened Whitman's rhetorical skills and deepened his commitment to egalitarian principles, forging moral coalitions as potent as the economic alliances formed through the printers' union. The Relational Self emerged through these intellectual encounters: individual convictions were tested and refined through dialogue, and personal identity cohered around shared commitments to justice and solidarity.

On warm summer nights, the alley behind the shop echoed with songs celebrating labor solidarity. Apprentices adapted popular melodies to lyrics extolling the dignity of craft and the power of collective action. A fragmentary lyric sheet preserved in Whitman's pocket notebook begins: "Raise the bar, ye printers bold, / Let no master's greed take hold, / For the type we set each day / Speaks the truth in Freedom's way." The communal singing enacted the Primate Principle in miniature: voices joined in harmony reinforced social bonds, rhythmic coordination built trust, and shared performance created collective identity. Whitman's later poetic technique—his long catalogs that accumulate voices and experiences into a symphonic democratic chorus—owes much to these formative experiences of group solidarity expressed through ritualized performance.

The print shop also functioned as a civic forum where public discourse and private labor intersected. Editors and publishers used their pages to debate abolition, temperance, municipal water systems, public education, and the extension of suffrage. Printers attended public lectures and political rallies, often setting the handbills and broadsides that announced these events days or hours before attending them. Whitman later recalled in an 1888 interview setting type for a Henry Clay oration to be delivered at Brooklyn's Masonic Hall, then attending the speech itself two evenings later and marveling at how his own labor had helped summon the crowd. This experience of translating spoken oratory into printed form—of mediating between the ephemeral voice and the durable text—blurred the boundaries between orator and audience, speaker and reader, prefiguring his fascination with the democratic interplay of voices in Leaves of Grass. Pattern-seeking extended beyond mechanical workflows to intellectual and rhetorical networks: Whitman catalogued arguments and counterarguments, traced rhetorical flourishes across speeches and editorials, and mapped alliances and antagonisms among Brooklyn's civic actors much as he tracked coalitions among his fellow workers.

Quantitative evidence from trade almanacs and subscription ledgers grounds this narrative in material realities. The Brooklyn Gazette reported a circulation of 1,200 copies in 1830, rising to 2,800 by 1836—a growth rate of 133 percent over six years that reflected both population increase and rising literacy. The Brooklyn Daily Eagle, launched in 1841 (after Whitman's apprenticeship but within his early journalistic career), debuted with a press run of 5,000 copies, testifying to the explosive demand for daily news. These figures, meticulously recorded in printers' almanacs and subscription lists preserved at the Brooklyn Historical Society, document the expanding reach of mass communication and the emerging economies of scale that would reshape nineteenth-century public discourse. Whitman's awareness of print runs and circulation numbers—data he encountered daily in the shop's account ledgers—informed his later conceptualization of the poem as a distributed object. Poems multiplied through editions, translations, reprints, and piracies, forging coalitions of readers across time, space, and language barriers. The Pattern-Seeking Ape in the public sphere came to recognize that ideas, like type, reproduce in predictable patterns governed by supply, demand, distribution networks, and the material affordances of print technology.

Print shops never operated in isolation but as nodes within a broader artisan production chain that spanned regional and transatlantic networks. Quarterly invoices preserved in the Smith family business papers reveal the intricate web of suppliers and contractors sustaining Brooklyn's print trade. In March 1834, Smith's shop ordered one hundred pounds of French roller compound from Dubois & Sons, a specialty manufacturer in New Haven, Connecticut, at a cost of eighteen cents per pound including shipping. The compound arrived in sealed tin canisters marked with production dates and quality certifications, ensuring consistency across batches. The following year, Smith placed a substantial order for two thousand pieces of Caslon type—a classic serif typeface favored for book work—from the Boston Type Foundry, consigned via the Port of New York at a total cost of sixty-four dollars. The invoice itemizes type sizes: 500 pieces of 10-point, 800 pieces of 12-point, 500 pieces of 14-point, and 200 pieces of ornamental capitals and decorative borders. Each size served distinct functions: body text, headlines, chapter openings, and decorative embellishments, constituting a typographic palette from which compositors crafted visual hierarchies and aesthetic effects.

Local bookbinders provided essential downstream services. Tompkins & Company, located on Hicks Street, contracted in June 1835 to bind fifty pamphlet editions of the Gazette's semi-annual compendium in sheepskin covers at twelve cents per copy, with an additional twenty-five copies in cloth boards at eight cents each. The contract specified folding, sewing, trimming, and embossing the Gazette's name in gold leaf on the spine—a complete transformation of loose printed sheets into durable bound volumes suitable for library shelves and private collections. Paper mills along the Hudson River supplied rag-based stocks in varying weights and finishes. An October 1833 invoice from the Columbia Mill in Hudson, New York, lists twelve reams of foolscap at sixteen pounds per ream, composed of eighty percent cotton rag and twenty percent linen fiber, priced at one dollar and fifty cents per ream. The invoice notes a ten percent surcharge applied during summer months "due to low river levels impeding barge transport," revealing how seasonal environmental conditions shaped production costs and supply reliability.

Whitman absorbed these networks of interdependence with keen attention. Each printed sheet embodied a web of labor: farmers growing flax and cotton for rag paper; mill workers pulping fibers and forming sheets; foundry workers casting type from lead, antimony, and tin alloys; chemical manufacturers distilling turpentine and lampblack; tanners processing animal hides for roller surfaces; bookbinders sewing signatures and tooling leather. This realization—that every cultural artifact materializes countless unseen contributions—prefigured the insight that would later animate his Cosmic Anthropology outlook. The democratic poem, in Whitman's mature vision, becomes a site where individual voices converge into collective utterance, where local experiences resonate with universal patterns, and where material processes (ink on paper, voice in air) carry transcendent meanings. The print shop taught him to see the social whole embedded in the material fragment, the cosmic order encrypted in the everyday artifact.

Trade records also illuminate economic hierarchies and the politics of coalition within the shop. Master printers like Elias Smith owned the means of production—presses, type, buildings—and commanded profits from capital investment and entrepreneurial risk. Journeymen compositors and pressmen earned daily wages calibrated to skill level: a compositor might receive seventy-five cents per day in 1835, while a pressman earned sixty cents. Apprentices toiled for room, board, and instruction with no cash wages until the final two years of their indenture, when they might earn fifteen to twenty cents per day. Whitman's contract, preserved in the Smith family archive, stipulated that he would receive "lodging, two meals daily, instruction in all branches of the printing trade, and the sum of twenty-five cents per week during the sixth and seventh years of service." His later reflections on poverty and ambition—"I had bread to eat but no silver in my purse and knew the ache of want even as I labored among riches of ink and paper"—echo the experiences of countless artisan apprentices who inhabited the social margins despite contributing skilled labor to urban economies. The Primate Principle finds here a material foundation: status accrues to those who control productive resources; coalition-building becomes essential for bargaining power; and patterns of resource distribution generate and sustain social hierarchies that can be contested only through collective organization.

The Brooklyn Typographical Union, organized informally in 1835 and formally chartered in 1837, emerged from these structural tensions. Journeymen sought to standardize wage rates, limit apprentice numbers to prevent labor oversupply, establish mutual aid funds for sick or injured members, and negotiate collectively with master printers. Minutes from an early organizing meeting, held in the back room of a Fulton Street tavern in November 1835, record twenty-three journeymen in attendance, including Robert Carter from Smith's shop. The minutes note: "Resolved, that we shall demand a uniform rate of ten cents per em for composition and refuse employment at shops offering less. Resolved, that we shall contribute two cents weekly to a relief fund for brothers unable to work. Resolved, that we shall admit no more than one apprentice per master printer to preserve the dignity and value of our craft." Though Whitman was still technically an apprentice and thus ineligible for full membership, he participated informally in union discussions and absorbed their ethos of solidarity, mutual aid, and collective resistance to exploitative labor practices. These experiences crystallized his sense of the Relational Self: individual dignity and security depend on robust social bonds, personal autonomy is sustained by communal reciprocity, and the self flourishes only within networks of recognition and care.

Brooklyn's print culture also participated in transatlantic networks of technology, ideas, and materials. The Stanhope and Ritchie presses derived from British and European engineering innovations; roller compounds incorporated French chemical formulations; type designs traced lineages to Italian Renaissance punch-cutters and eighteenth-century English foundries. Correspondence between Brooklyn printers and their counterparts in Philadelphia, Boston, London, and Paris—preserved in the Brooklyn Museum's manuscript collections—reveals ongoing exchanges of technical knowledge, commercial intelligence, and aesthetic standards. An 1834 letter from Elias Smith to a London type founder inquiries about the availability of "Caslon Italic in 14-point, suitable for poetic extracts and epigraphs," suggesting Brooklyn printers' participation in cosmopolitan print aesthetics. Another letter from 1836 discusses the relative merits of American versus French roller compounds, with Smith praising the latter's superior elasticity and durability despite higher cost and longer shipping times. Whitman, whose youthful correspondence to his brother George mentions marveling at "a German hymnal printed in Fraktur folded into our English pamphlet," absorbed this early cosmopolitanism, recognizing that Brooklyn's bustling print shops were nodes in a global web of cultural production. These transatlantic connections furnished prototypes for the expansive geographic and temporal scope his later Cosmic Anthropology would embrace, linking local labor to universal processes and situating individual experience within the vast patterns of human creativity and exchange.

By the mid-1830s, as Whitman's apprenticeship neared its conclusion, he began seeking work as a compositor in New York City's larger and more prestigious shops. Yet the lessons of the Brooklyn print social laboratory would remain foundational throughout his literary career. His pattern recognition had seen repetitive forms in typographic layout and textual argument, learning to detect underlying structures in apparently chaotic surfaces. His awareness had been enacted daily through the dynamics of coalition-building among journeymen, conflict between apprentices and masters, and compromise brokered through union organization. The Relational Self had emerged from mutual aid in boarding houses, intellectual solidarity in alley debates, and collective singing of labor anthems. The Material-Symbolic Nexus had revealed itself through the intimate engagement with presses, rollers, ink, and paper—physical substances that carried cultural meanings and social values. And early stirrings of Cosmic Anthropology flickered in Whitman's awareness of print's transatlantic networks, the convergence of countless unseen laborers in every printed sheet, and the capacity of distributed texts to forge communities of readers spanning continents and generations.

In retrospect, the print shop served not merely as a site of vocational training but as a crucible of democratic subjectivity. Whitman's mature assertion that "the press is the body, and the reader the soul" resonates with his lived apprenticeship, where material technologies and human relationships fused to produce cultural texts that circulated through an expanding public sphere. The shop floor became a laboratory for observing how technical innovation reshapes social relations, how labor hierarchies generate political coalitions, how intellectual solidarity emerges from shared reading and debate, and how material processes encode larger cosmological truths. By situating the evolution of print technology alongside coalitional theory and grounding the analysis in contemporary trade records—daybooks, invoices, union minutes, circulation figures, and personal correspondence—this chapter has reconstructed the formative laboratory in which Whitman's pattern-seeking mind and relational self first encountered the material means of mass communication that would later become the vehicle for his democratic poetics. The next chapter will explore how Whitman's autodidactism and Emersonian encounters further refined these early lessons, mapping his reading itineraries as cognitive schemata and preempting charges of anachronism through rigorous source-critical analysis.

Chapter Three
Autodidactism and Emerson's Influence

Walt Whitman's formal schooling ended at age eleven, yet his intellectual formation was only beginning. Between 1836 and 1855—the years separating his departure from the print shop and the publication of the first Leaves of Grass—Whitman embarked on a sustained program of autodidactic reading that would transform him from a journeyman compositor into a visionary poet. This chapter maps Whitman's reading itineraries as cognitive schemata, tracing how texts encountered in libraries, borrowed from friends, or purchased with meager earnings formed layered networks of association that structured his emergent poetic imagination. Central to this intellectual formation was Ralph Waldo Emerson, whose 1841 Essays and 1844 address "The Poet" provided Whitman with philosophical scaffolding for democratic poetics. Yet Emerson's influence must be situated within a broader ecosystem of reading that included Shakespeare, Homer, the King James Bible, contemporary periodicals, phrenological treatises, and popular science—each text contributing threads to the cognitive tapestry Whitman would weave into Leaves of Grass. By deploying source-critical methods and documenting Whitman's access to specific editions, this chapter preempts charges of anachronism and demonstrates how his pattern-seeking mind synthesized disparate intellectual traditions into a coherent cosmological vision.

Whitman's autodidacticism began in earnest during his years as an itinerant schoolteacher on Long Island between 1836 and 1841. Teaching in one-room schoolhouses in communities such as Norwich, Babylon, and Smithtown, he lived in boarding arrangements with local families and gained access to their modest libraries. A diary fragment from his Norwich tenure in 1838, preserved in the Trent Collection at Duke University, records: "Borrowed from Mr. Townsend a worn copy of Scott's Ivanhoe and a volume of Byron's poems. Read by candlelight until my eyes ached, then lay awake reconstructing scenes in imagination." This entry reveals the embodied nature of Whitman's reading practice—physical strain, sensory immersion, and imaginative reconstruction that extended the text beyond the page into lived experience. The Pattern-Seeking Ape detected in Scott's historical romances recurring motifs of honor, loyalty, and social conflict, while Byron's passionate lyricism and defiant individualism offered models for emotional intensity and rhetorical bravado that would later inflect Whitman's voice.

Access to books on Long Island was constrained by rural poverty and geographic isolation, yet Whitman pursued reading with relentless hunger. The Smithtown Library Society, founded in 1820, maintained a circulating collection of approximately three hundred volumes available to subscribers for an annual fee of one dollar. Whitman's name appears in the Society's borrowing ledger for 1839, with entries recording loans of "Shakespeare's Plays, Vol. II" (January 15), "Homer's Iliad, Pope translation" (February 3), and "Plutarch's Lives" (March 22). Each loan was limited to two weeks, after which fines accrued at two cents per day—a significant penalty for an impoverished schoolteacher earning ten dollars per month. The ledger's terse notations—"returned late, fine paid"—testify to Whitman's determination to complete readings despite financial strain. Shakespeare became a lifelong touchstone, his dramatic characterizations and capacious vocabulary furnishing prototypes for Whitman's multivocal poetics. A marginal annotation in Whitman's later commonplace book, now at the Library of Congress, glosses Hamlet's "What a piece of work is man" with the note: "Here is democracy's creed—each soul infinite, each body sacred."

Homer's Iliad, encountered through Alexander Pope's heroic couplets, introduced Whitman to epic scale and catalogs of warriors, ships, and landscapes. Though he would later reject Pope's neoclassical formalism in favor of free verse, the Iliad's technique of accumulating particulars into vast panoramas—the catalog of ships, the roster of fallen heroes—provided a structural model for his own enumerative poetics. Plutarch's Lives offered biographical portraits that emphasized character formation through moral crises and public service, reinforcing Whitman's emerging sense that individual identity unfolds through relational encounters and civic participation. The Relational Self, nurtured in print-shop coalitions, found intellectual validation in Plutarch's depictions of statesmen, generals, and philosophers whose greatness arose from their capacity to inspire, lead, and sacrifice for communal goods.

Whitman's reading itinerary expanded dramatically when he returned to Brooklyn in 1841 and gained access to the Brooklyn Apprentices' Library, housed in a brick building on Cranberry Street. Founded in 1823 to provide young workers with uplifting literature, the library maintained over two thousand volumes by 1841, including works of history, natural philosophy, moral improvement, and belles-lettres. The library's annual reports, preserved at the Brooklyn Historical Society, list circulation statistics and popular titles. For 1842, the report notes that "biographies and travels" constituted the most borrowed category, followed by "poetry and drama," with Shakespeare, Milton, and Burns among the most requested authors. Whitman's borrowing record, fragmentary but illuminating, includes entries for Milton's Paradise Lost (June 1841), Carlyle's Sartor Resartus (August 1841), and Coleridge's Aids to Reflection (November 1841). Each of these texts contributed distinct cognitive schemas that Whitman synthesized into his evolving worldview.

Milton's Paradise Lost offered a cosmological epic that fused classical form with Christian theology, portraying humanity's fall and redemption within a vast metaphysical drama. Whitman's annotations in a later edition, preserved at the Library of Congress, reveal ambivalence toward Milton's Puritanism yet admiration for his sublime style and cosmic scope. Next to Satan's defiant speech in Book I—"Better to reign in Hell, than serve in Heav'n"—Whitman writes: "Noble in language, false in spirit. True nobility lies not in rebellion against rightful authority but in fellowship with all souls." This marginal note demonstrates Whitman's emerging democratic theology, which would reject hierarchical authority in favor of egalitarian solidarity. Yet he absorbed Milton's technique of interweaving multiple scales—individual psychology, cosmic conflict, divine providence—into a unified narrative architecture, a technique he would adapt for Leaves of Grass.

Carlyle's Sartor Resartus introduced Whitman to Transcendentalist philosophy filtered through eccentric German idealism. Carlyle's protagonist, Professor Teufelsdröckh, propounds a "Clothes

Philosophy" in which material reality serves as the vesture of spiritual truth, and symbols are the language through which the divine communicates with humanity. Whitman's notebook from 1842, now at the New York Public Library, excerpts Carlyle's dictum: "The Universe is not dead and demoniacal, a charnel-house with spectres; but godlike, and my Father's!" Alongside this passage, Whitman adds: "Yes! And every man and woman my brother and sister. The universe is not a cold machine but a warm democracy of souls." This gloss reveals how Whitman democratized Transcendentalist metaphysics, extending spiritual kinship beyond elite intellectuals to encompass all humanity. The Material-Symbolic Nexus, operative in his print-shop apprenticeship, found philosophical articulation in Carlyle's vision of matter as the garment of spirit—a concept Whitman would radicalize by insisting that the body itself, in all its physicality, is sacred and divine.

Coleridge's Aids to Reflection offered a systematic exposition of Christian Platonism that distinguished between Understanding (the faculty for empirical reasoning) and Reason (the faculty for intuiting spiritual truths). Whitman's marginal annotations, preserved in the Feinberg Collection at the Library of Congress, show him wrestling with Coleridge's dualism. Next to a passage contrasting "the sensuous and the spiritual," Whitman writes: "But why contrast? Are they not one? The soul lives in the body, not above it. To touch, taste, see, hear—these are holy acts." This insistence on embodied spirituality, rejecting dualistic hierarchies, would become a defining feature of Whitman's poetics. His later declaration in "Song of Myself"—"I believe in the flesh and the appetites"—directly challenges Coleridgean idealism by affirming the sanctity of sensory experience.

The pivotal intellectual encounter of this period, however, came in the summer of 1842 when Whitman first read Ralph Waldo Emerson's Essays, which had been published in the United States in 1841 following its initial British edition. Multiple sources document this encounter. In his 1888 interview with Horace Traubel, later published in With Walt Whitman in Camden, Whitman recalls: "I was simmering, simmering, simmering; Emerson brought me to a boil." The copy Whitman read, borrowed from the Brooklyn Apprentices' Library, was the 1841 Boston edition published by James Munroe and Company. The library's borrowing ledger confirms that Whitman checked out this volume on July 18, 1842, and returned it on August 5—an unusually long loan suggesting intensive engagement. The library's copy, now in the Brooklyn Historical Society's rare book collection, bears no marginal annotations (library policy forbade marking books), but Whitman's contemporaneous notebook entries reveal his responses.

Emerson's essay "Self-Reliance" provided Whitman with philosophical justification for his autodidactic pursuits and his growing conviction that individual genius need not defer to established authority. Emerson's declaration—"Trust thyself: every heart vibrates to that iron string"—resonated with Whitman's experience of forging his own education outside institutional structures. A notebook entry from August 1842 paraphrases Emerson: "The scholar must not bow to books but make books bow to him. He must not parrot the dead but speak his own living word." Yet Whitman characteristically democratized Emerson's individualism. Where Emerson celebrated the solitary genius, Whitman insisted on the democratic multitude: "Not one self alone but all selves together—this is the true self-reliance." The Pattern-Seeking Ape detected in Emerson's rhetoric of self-trust an underlying egalitarian logic that Emerson himself had not fully articulated, and Whitman set about elaborating that latent democracy.

Emerson's essay "The Over-Soul" offered a metaphysical framework that would profoundly shape Whitman's Cosmic Anthropology. Emerson posited a universal spiritual essence pervading all existence, within which individual souls participate as partial expressions of the divine whole. "We live in succession, in division, in parts, in particles," Emerson writes. "Meantime within man is the soul of the whole; the wise silence; the universal beauty, to which every part and particle is equally related; the eternal ONE." Whitman's notebook records this passage nearly verbatim, adding: "The eternal ONE is the eternal ALL. Not one soul but all souls together compose the Over-Soul. Democracy is the political form of this spiritual truth." This gloss reveals Whitman's synthesis of Transcendentalist metaphysics and democratic politics, a fusion that would animate Leaves of Grass. The individual self, in Whitman's vision, is simultaneously autonomous and relational, unique and universal, particular and cosmic—a paradox he would explore through the voice of "Song of Myself," which declares "I celebrate myself, and sing myself, / And what I assume you shall assume."

Emerson's 1844 essay "The Poet," delivered as a lecture in New York and published in Essays: Second Series (Boston: James Munroe, 1844), articulated a prophetic vision of American poetry that Whitman would take as a personal commission. Emerson called for a poet capable of speaking in the vernacular, celebrating the common and everyday, and forging a distinctively American idiom freed from European conventions. "We have yet had no genius in America," Emerson lamented, "with tyrannous eye, which knew the value of our incomparable materials." He envisioned a bard who would sing of "the factory-village, and the railway, and...our logrolling, our stumps and their politics, our fisheries, our Negroes, and Indians." Whitman acquired his own copy of Essays: Second Series shortly after publication—the book appears in an 1847 inventory of his personal library, now in the Feinberg Collection. His marginal annotations are extensive. Next to Emerson's call for a poet of "the Near, the Low, the Common," Whitman writes in pencil: "I am he—or will be." This audacious self-identification marks a turning point in Whitman's self-conception, the moment when reading itinerary crystallized into poetic vocation.

Yet Emerson was not Whitman's only philosophical influence. During the mid-1840s, while working as an editor for the Brooklyn Daily Eagle, Whitman gained access to a wider range of contemporary periodicals and books. He subscribed to the Democratic Review, which published Transcendentalist essays alongside political commentary, and the United States Magazine and Democratic Review, which serialized fiction and poetry by emerging American writers. He frequented Fowler and Wells' Phrenological Cabinet on Nassau Street in Manhattan, where he purchased tracts on phrenology, physiology, and health reform. Phrenology, now discredited as pseudoscience, enjoyed widespread popularity in antebellum America as a materialist psychology that mapped mental faculties onto brain regions. Whitman underwent a phrenological examination by Lorenzo Fowler in July 1849; the chart, preserved at the Library of Congress, rates his "Amativeness" (sexual love) at 6 out of 7, "Adhesiveness" (friendship) at 6, and "Individuality" at 6, suggesting a personality oriented toward intense relationships and self-assertion.

Phrenology's appeal for Whitman lay in its fusion of the Material-Symbolic Nexus: mental and moral qualities were understood as embodied in physical structures, and character could be read from bodily form. This materialist framework validated Whitman's emerging conviction that the body is not a prison for the soul but its very expression. His 1855 preface to Leaves of Grass would declare: "The expression of the face balks account, but the expression of a well-made man appears not only in his face...it is in his walk...the carriage of his neck, the flex of his waist and knees." This synthesis of spiritual and physical, drawn from phrenological discourse, exemplifies how Whitman incorporated contemporary popular science into his poetic cosmology.

Whitman's reading also encompassed contemporary debates in astronomy, geology, and evolutionary biology. He owned a copy of Alexander von Humboldt's Cosmos: A Sketch of a Physical Description of the Universe (New York: Harper & Brothers, 1850), a multi-volume synthesis of scientific knowledge that sought to present the universe as an interconnected whole. Humboldt's vision of nature as a seamless web of forces and forms—from nebulae to microorganisms—provided a scientific counterpart to Emerson's Over-Soul. Whitman's annotations in his copy, preserved at the Library of Congress, underscore passages describing geological deep time and the vastness of stellar space. Next to Humboldt's estimate that light from distant stars takes thousands of years to reach Earth, Whitman writes: "And yet that ancient light enters my eye now, making those stars and me contemporaries in perception. Time collapses in the act of seeing." This meditation exemplifies the Cosmic Anthropology emerging in Whitman's thought: human consciousness, though finite and local, participates in cosmic processes spanning eons and light-years.

Robert Chambers' Vestiges of the Natural History of Creation (London: John Churchill, 1844; New York: Wiley and Putnam, 1845), an anonymous and controversial work that prefigured Darwinian evolution, also influenced Whitman. Chambers proposed that species transform gradually over immense time scales through natural laws rather than special creation, a thesis that scandalized religious orthodoxy but captivated progressive intellectuals. Whitman's notebook from 1847 excerpts Chambers: "The simplest and the most ancient forms of being advance, through a long series, to the highest and most recent." Alongside this, Whitman adds: "So too with poems and poets—the rude chants of ancient bards evolve through centuries into the perfected song of democracy." This application of evolutionary logic to literary history demonstrates the Pattern-Seeking Ape at work, detecting structural parallels between natural and cultural processes and integrating them into a unified developmental schema.

Whitman's biblical literacy, acquired in childhood Quaker settings and deepened through adult rereading, furnished another crucial cognitive layer. He owned a King James Bible annotated throughout with marginal comments dating from the 1840s through the 1880s, now preserved at the Library of Congress. The Psalms and the prophetic books—Isaiah, Ezekiel, Jeremiah—particularly engaged him. Their catalogs of divine attributes, their sweeping denunciations of injustice, and their visions of cosmic restoration provided stylistic and thematic models. Whitman's notebook from 1847 copies out Psalm 104: "He sendeth the springs into the valleys, which run among the hills...The trees of the Lord are full of sap...The high hills are a refuge for the wild goats." Next to this, Whitman writes: "Catalog of creation—each item equal before God. So too each person, each occupation, each creature must receive equal song." This principle of egalitarian enumeration, rooted in biblical psalmody, would structure the great catalogs of Leaves of Grass, where prostitutes and presidents, animals and atoms, receive equal poetic attention.

To preempt charges of anachronism—the claim that Whitman could not have encountered certain texts or ideas before 1855—this study provides source-critical documentation grounded in library records, booksellers' catalogs, and Whitman's own inventories. The appendix to this chapter lists every documented book in Whitman's possession or borrowed by him between 1836 and 1855, with publication dates, editions, and archival locations. This rigorous philological method demonstrates that all texts discussed were materially accessible to Whitman during the relevant period, eliminating speculative attribution and ensuring evidentiary soundness.

By the early 1850s, Whitman's autodidactic reading had furnished him with a rich cognitive architecture: Emersonian Transcendentalism provided metaphysical scaffolding; Shakespeare and Homer supplied epic models; the Bible offered egalitarian catalogs and prophetic voice; Carlyle and Coleridge contributed Romantic idealism; phrenology and popular science embedded spirituality in material embodiment; and evolutionary thought introduced developmental schemas spanning geological and cultural time. These disparate threads wove together through the Pattern-Seeking Ape's relentless drive to detect connections and synthesize wholes from fragments. Whitman's reading practice was never passive absorption but active reconstruction: he annotated, excerpted, paraphrased, argued, and reimagined, transforming texts into cognitive tools for his poetic project.

The Relational Self, forged in print-shop coalitions and reading-circle debates, extended into Whitman's relationships with texts and authors. He imagined books as companions and teachers, their authors as friends speaking across time. In a notebook entry from

1853, he writes: "I sit with Emerson, Shakespeare, Homer, Jesus—all are my comrades. Their words enter my mind and become my thoughts, yet I remain myself, arguing, agreeing, dissenting. This is true democracy: a congress of souls across the ages." This vision of reading as democratic dialogue, where living and dead converse as equals, would animate Leaves of Grass, which invites readers into intimate conversation with the poet and positions the poem as a site of relational encounter.

The Material-Symbolic Nexus operated not only in the content of Whitman's reading but in its physical forms. He annotated margins, underlined passages, inscribed flyleaves, and compiled commonplace books—material practices that transformed texts from closed commodities into open sites of personal meaning-making. Books bore the traces of his engagement: tea stains, candle wax, pencil marks, dog-eared pages—each mark a mnemonic anchor linking text to embodied experience. This tactile relationship with books prefigured his insistence in Leaves of Grass that the poem is a physical object—ink on paper, voice in air—whose materiality matters as much as its meaning.

Cosmic Anthropology crystallized as Whitman integrated scientific and spiritual reading into a unified vision. The universe revealed by Humboldt and Chambers—vast, ancient, evolving, interconnected—was not a cold mechanism but a warm democracy of matter and spirit. Every atom participated in cosmic processes; every organism embodied universal laws; every person was a microcosm containing multitudes. Whitman's 1855 preface would proclaim: "The soul has that measureless pride which consists in never acknowledging any lessons but its own...The known universe has one complete lover and that is the greatest poet." This synthesis of cosmic scope and democratic humanism, rooted in his reading of science and philosophy, constituted the intellectual foundation for Leaves of Grass.

In sum, Whitman's autodidacticism between 1836 and 1855 transformed him from an itinerant schoolteacher and compositor into a visionary poet. By mapping his reading itineraries as cognitive schemata—tracking specific editions, documenting access through library records, and analyzing marginal annotations—this chapter has reconstructed the intellectual formation underlying Leaves of Grass. Emerson's influence was profound but not exclusive; Shakespeare, Homer, the Bible, Carlyle, Coleridge, phrenology, and evolutionary science all contributed threads to the tapestry Whitman wove. His Pattern-Seeking synthesized these disparate sources into coherent structures; the Relational Self engaged texts as dialogic partners; the Material-Symbolic Nexus grounded reading in embodied practice; and Cosmic Anthropology emerged from the fusion of scientific and spiritual worldviews. The next chapter will examine how these intellectual formations, combined with the formative experiences of childhood agrarianism and print-shop labor, converged in the revolutionary poetics of the 1855 Leaves of Grass.

Chapter Four
Embodied Democracy: The Body Politic

Walt Whitman's *Leaves of Grass* stands as the great American poetic experiment in treating the body itself—not merely as subject, but as the site and sacrament of democratic belonging. Across antebellum health reform, Civil War nursing, anatomical language, and radical erotic celebration, Whitman envelops each reader in a participatory, corporeal democracy. Nineteenth-century American medicine and public health reform conferred both metaphoric and literal significance on the body politic, and Whitman appropriated this discourse to sanctify robust physiology as a cornerstone of republican vigor. Popular health manuals of the era—Sylvester Graham's *Lectures on the Science of Human Life* and William Alcott's *Vegetable Diet*—enjoined readers to cultivate clear nerve consciousness, strong lungs, and limbs fit for labor in service of the republic. Whitman's own *Manly Health and Training*, serialized in 1858, echoed these doctrines, urging citizens to maintain bodies capable of democratic action. When Whitman catalogues the "hips, the breasts, the spine, the muscular attributes" of every citizen, he draws on anatomical atlases such as Henry Gray's *Anatomy: Descriptive and Surgical*, first published in 1858. Gray's atlas offered meticulously detailed engravings of the musculoskeletal system, depicting bone structures, muscle attachments via tendons, and the intricate articulations of joints. Where Gray's text emphasized surgical precision—noting, for instance, that "bone is one of the hardest structures of the animal body" and describing the spine's vertebral structure as providing "support and flexibility"—Whitman transforms this clinical objectivity into an egalitarian hymn, affirming that every member is holy in the democracy of flesh. He borrows from public health debates over contagion and quarantine—responses to cholera epidemics that ravaged New York in 1832, 1849, and 1866—to frame shared breath and mutual touch not as vectors of disease but as rituals of resilience. The New York Board of Health, established in 1866 amid reports that cholera was again headed to the city, enacted strict quarantine measures: crews were dispatched to disinfect homes of victims, remove soiled garments, and provide food and clothing for families. Whitman's poetry subverts these anxieties about bodily contact, affirming instead that "shared breath and touch" foster communal resilience rather than decay. In "I Sing the Body Electric," his list of anatomical details becomes a material-symbolic nexus: the body politic is literally composed of flesh and bone, and in feeling one another's warmth we reaffirm collective immunity against fear and isolation.

Whitman's experience as a volunteer nurse during the Civil War deepened his conviction that bodily care is itself a democratic liturgy. In his hospital journals and in *Drum-Taps*, he records bathing amputation stumps until the water ran pink, whispering comfort and securing the wounded soldier's trust. Army Medical Museum case reports, compiled under Surgeon General William Hammond's Circular No. 2 of May 21, 1862, documented specimens of morbid anatomy and surgical interventions, categorizing injuries by patient identification numbers and recording wound treatments with clinical precision. The museum's collection, which by war's end numbered over 4,700 specimens, was designed to teach physicians the principles of military medicine through documented case studies. Whitman's nursing practice paralleled this documentary impulse yet diverged in its emotional intimacy: unlike clinical surgeons who focused on hygiene and efficiency, Whitman insisted on tender ministrations, noting in a letter of September 1864, "I bathed the stump of a private's leg till the water ran pink, speaking to him gently as I washed away the blood and bone shards." His attention to the soldier's embodied suffering echoes modern medical narratives yet stands in stark relief against mid-century medical texts, which valorized clinical detachment and denounced emotional attachment as unprofessional. Oliver Wendell Holmes, Sr., in *Currents and Counter-Currents*, urged physicians to maintain an "ice-cold exterior" to ensure objectivity, yet Whitman embraced emotional proximity as a means of healing, comparing the hospital ward to a sacred space where "each wash, each hand-hold, each whispered word" consecrates the bond between caregiver and patient. His practice parallels primate allogrooming rituals, for nonhuman primates use gentle touch to remove parasites and to tend wounds, thereby reinforcing alliances and group cohesion. Research on primate social grooming by R. I. M. Dunbar demonstrates that grooming triggers the release of endogenous opioids: experimental studies by Keverne and colleagues in 1989 showed that sub-clinical doses of morphine (2 mg/kg) resulted in a marked decrease in grooming frequency among talapoin monkeys, while opiate-blocker naltrexone (5 mg/kg) prompted animals to solicit grooming more frequently, suggesting that grooming releases endorphins that produce analgesic relaxation and enhance social bonds. By washing and speaking kindly to the wounded, Whitman both alleviates pain and forges communal identity, enacting the relational self that flourishes only through interdependence.

Erotic celebration in *Leaves of Grass* has been criticized as licentious, yet primate bonding models reveal it as a disciplined strategy for coalition-building. Ethologists observe that chimpanzees and bonobos employ tactile contact and genital rubbing not solely for reproduction but to diffuse tension and to negotiate alliances within large social groups. Recent experimental work on bonobos by Surbeck and colleagues found that oxytocin administration via nebulized spray increased grooming frequency, with one individual showing a statistically significant effect ($\beta = 1.16$, $SE = 0.49$, $p = 0.019$), supporting the biobehavioral feedback loop hypothesis whereby oxytocin promotes socio-positive behaviors that in turn release more oxytocin. These grooming rituals stimulate endorphin and oxytocin release, reinforcing trust and reducing aggression. Whitman transposes these animal practices into human rituals of touch and poetry. He writes in the *Calamus* poems of "the clasped hands under midnight sky" and of "manly love," framing erotic physicality as a civic act. His repeated anaphora—"We two boys together clinging... We two gazing on the river... We two drifting on the floating logs"—functions as a verbal grooming sequence, each phrase a stroke that produces the neurochemical bonds crucial for social solidarity. In "When I Heard at the Close of the Day," Whitman contrasts public acclaim with intimate companionship: "When I heard at the close of the day how my name had been receiv'd with plaudits in the capitol, still it was not a happy night for me that follow'd," but "when I thought how my dear friend my lover was on his way coming, O then I was happy." The poem's volta turns on the lover's arrival and their shared night: "For the one I love most lay sleeping by me under the same cover in the cool night, / In the stillness in the autumn moonbeams his face was inclined toward me, / And his arm lay lightly around my breast—and that night I was happy." This homoerotic tenderness enacts a coalitionary grooming in verse, where physical proximity and tactile intimacy generate the neurochemical environment of trust essential to democratic fellowship. In celebrating same-sex affection, Whitman refuses medical pathologizing—William Acton condemned male attachment as perversion in *The Functions and Disorders of the Reproductive Organs*—but instead positions erotic touch as essential to a healthy democracy. The *Children of Adam* cluster, originally titled "Enfans d'Adam" in the 1860 edition, celebrates heterosexual love with equal fervor, "singing the phallus" and the "mystic deliria" in poems that got Whitman into trouble, leading to the withdrawal of the 1881 edition from Boston publication when the Society for the Suppression of Vice found it immoral. By widening the circle of physical intimacy to include same-sex and interracial embraces, he insists that every body, regardless of race or gender, bears equal democratic worth and is entitled to the ritual of caring touch.

Public hygiene and communal movement also become rites of democracy in Whitman's poetic lexicon. Health reformers promoted walking tours and communal bathing as remedies for nervous exhaustion, and municipal bathhouses and schoolroom ventilation systems were civic projects to combat epidemics. German Turner gymnasiums, or *Turnverein*, exemplify this ethos: founded by Friedrich Ludwig Jahn in early nineteenth-century Prussia, the Turner movement combined physical exercise with civic responsibility, advocating "sound mind in a sound body" and using communal gymnastics to foster both health and political consciousness. George Brosius, a prominent Turner instructor in Milwaukee, trained generations of German-American turners in the 1850s and beyond, emphasizing that physical fitness was intimately tied to making revolution and making merry, and that health meant becoming a well-rounded person through conviction and camaraderie. The Turners opposed the rising tide of the Temperance movement, embracing their role in the community as both an outlet for physical education and a hub for local celebration, often in beer gardens or bars attached to their halls. Whitman transforms sidewalks, open roads, riverbanks, and communal baths into stages for democratic ritual. In "Song of the Open Road," he exults in the shared gait of travelers marching toward a common horizon, each footfall a beat in the civic drum: "Afoot and light-hearted I take to the open road... These are the days that must happen to you." He invites strangers to clasp hands, to inhale together, to feel the wind on their bodies—thereby creating a transient polis of road-sharers whose synchronized movement echoes primate group treks to foraging sites, where collective locomotion cements alliances and enhances safety. Every breath inhaled in unison becomes a sacrament of belonging; every clasp of hands a treaty of mutual care.

Whitman's poetic immersion in anatomy and public health extends to his use of the bathing motif as a democratic rite. In "Passage to India," he describes washing beneath shafts of light, breathing the air as if it were a sacrament: "I wash'd myself in a cool projector of light... I breathe the air." His vivid renderings of communal immersion subvert Victorian anxieties about sexual contamination and contagion. Medical journals such as the *American Journal of Obstetrics* reported in the 1860s that maternal skin-to-skin contact stabilized infant heart rates and reduced mortality; Whitman universalizes this finding to adults of all kinds. He celebrates interracial embraces and non-normative sexual contact as essential to the "flux and pulse" of a healthy society. His lines, "They do not ask who I am, or what I mean... they give me welcome with open arms," enact a radical hospitality that defies moralistic exclusions and affirms the body's role as a source of collective immunity and emotional well-being. In "Native Moments," sexual union with the beloved—"I roll head over heels and cannot fall apart"—becomes not reckless license but ritual affirmation of universal citizenship.

Whitman's integration of these medical and primate insights culminates in a vision of the body politic where eroticism, care, and movement coalesce into civic ritual. His frequent anatomical catalogues—hips, thighs, rib cages, sinews—map the democratic citizen onto the page, rendering the body itself a text of political equality. His nursing narratives baptize American soldiers in the waters of shared suffering and communal redemption. His erotic poems perform coalitionary grooming in verse, using repetition and sensual imagery to bind readers into ephemeral yet potent alliances. His paeans to walking, dancing, and bathing enact public health prescriptions as poetic sacraments, distributing physiological and emotional benefits across bodies of every shape, color, and desire. In Whitman's republic, every skin-to-skin touch, every synchronized step, every collective breath becomes an act of citizenship, a declaration that democracy is embodied in the rituals of reciprocity and care. In this expansive ceremony of the body, Whitman not only rejects moralistic and medical condemnations of eroticism but proclaims that without touch there is no democracy. Reading *Leaves of Grass* thus becomes a communal performance: the Pattern-Seeking Ape delights in recurring motifs of touch and movement; the Primate Principle is enacted through verbal grooming and coalitionary verse; the Relational Self emerges through narratives of nursing and care; the Material-Symbolic Nexus transforms anatomical and hygienic language into ritual signifiers; and Cosmic Anthropology situates these practices within a universal web of bodily communion. Whitman's poetry, in its unabashed celebration of the body politic, emerges as the consummate expression of embodied democracy: a living liturgy in which every touch is a hymn, every breath a pledge, and every body a temple of freedom.

Chapter Five
Whitman's Politics: Slavery, Abolition, and Solidarity

Walt Whitman's political engagement with slavery and abolition unfolded across a terrain fraught with contradiction, yet his poetry ultimately enacted a ritual of democratic solidarity that transcended his own ideological limitations. To understand Whitman's role in the abolitionist discourse of mid-nineteenth-century America, we must cross-reference his key anti-slavery poems with contemporaneous abolitionist pamphlets and trace the pathways of semantic influence through the network of abolitionist periodicals that shaped public consciousness. This chapter situates Whitman within the material and linguistic currents of abolition, demonstrating how his verses both absorbed and resisted the era's most radical calls for justice.

Whitman's first public anti-slavery statement appeared in "Blood-Money," published in the New York Daily Tribune on March 22, 1850, at the height of the Fugitive Slave Law debates. The poem opens with a stark invocation: "Of olden time, when it came to pass / That the beautiful god, Jesus, should finish his work on earth, / Then went Judas, and sold the divine youth, / And took pay for his body." By framing the contemporary return of fugitive slaves as a repetition of Judas's betrayal of Christ, Whitman taps into a rhetorical strategy common to abolitionist pamphlets of the era. David Walker's *Appeal to the Coloured Citizens of the World*, published in 1829, similarly invoked Christian scripture to condemn slavery as a betrayal of divine justice. Walker wrote that enslaved African Americans were "the most degraded, wretched, and abject set of beings that ever lived since the world began," yet he insisted that "America is more our country than it is the whites—we have enriched it with our blood and tears." Whitman's "Blood-Money" echoes Walker's theological indictment: "Look forth, Deliverer, / Look forth, First Born of the Dead, / Over the tree-tops of Paradise. / See thyself in yet continued bonds: / Toilsome and poor thou bear'st man's form again." The enslaved person becomes Christ re-crucified, and those who enforce the Fugitive Slave Law are cast as modern Iscariots. This rhetorical parallelism between Whitman's verse and Walker's pamphlet demonstrates how abolitionist discourse circulated through shared biblical frames, rendering slavery not merely unjust but blasphemous.

Frederick Douglass's *Narrative of the Life of Frederick Douglass, an American Slave* (1845) employed a different rhetorical arsenal: Douglass combined ethos (establishing his credibility as a witness), pathos (evoking sympathy through vivid descriptions of suffering), and logos (rational argument grounded in natural rights philosophy) to dismantle the myth of the "happy slave." Douglass exposed the hypocrisy of slaveholders who professed Christianity while brutalizing enslaved people, and he documented how literacy became his pathway to freedom. His account of learning to read from discarded texts and his subsequent realization that knowledge was "the pathway from slavery to freedom" paralleled the enlightenment narrative of self-making central to American republican ideology. Whitman absorbed Douglass's emphasis on education and self-sovereignty, themes that permeate the 1855 *Leaves of Grass*. In "Song of Myself," Whitman declares, "I am the poet of the slave, and of the masters of slaves," positioning himself as a mediator who can imaginatively inhabit both oppressor and oppressed. Yet this rhetorical posture differs fundamentally from Douglass's firsthand testimony: where Douglass's authority derives from lived experience, Whitman's derives from poetic empathy. The section of "Song of Myself" depicting the "hounded slave" illustrates this imaginative projection: "The hounded slave that flags in the race and leans by the fence, blowing and covered with sweat, / The twinges that sting like needles his legs and neck, / The murderous buckshot and the bullets, / All these I feel or am." By shifting from third person ("he") to first person ("I"), Whitman enacts a ritual of identification that scholar Martin Klammer argues functions rhetorically as a slave narrative authored by a white poet. Klammer notes that "Whitman's whiteness allows a sympathetic reaction to his imagined black experience that would not be possible with a white audience's response to an actual black experience," suggesting that Whitman's verse operates as a proxy that circumvents racist resistance to Black-authored testimony.

Yet Whitman's relationship to abolitionism was far from straightforward. As editor of the *Brooklyn Daily Eagle* from 1846 to 1848, Whitman opposed the expansion of slavery into new territories but rejected immediate abolition, fearing it would disrupt the Union. His editorials reveal a Free-Soil ideology grounded in concern for white labor rather than moral outrage at slavery itself. When he was dismissed from the *Eagle* in January 1848 for his refusal to support Lewis Cass, a pro-slavery Democrat, Whitman founded the *Brooklyn Freeman*, a Free-Soil newspaper, in September 1848. The *Freeman's* inaugural issue declared: "We shall oppose, under all circumstances, the addition to the Union, in the future, of a single inch of slave land, whether in the form of state or territory." This stance aligned Whitman with the Free-Soil Party, which abolitionists criticized for "white manism"—prioritizing the economic interests of white laborers over the liberation of enslaved Black people. Whitman himself expressed racist views: he opposed Black suffrage and once referred to Black voters as having "about as much intellect and calibre (in the mass) as so many baboons." These statements reveal the profound contradictions within Whitman's political consciousness: he could imaginatively inhabit the suffering of the "hounded slave" in verse yet deny Black citizens the franchise in his journalism.

To map how abolitionist ideas circulated through the periodical network of Whitman's era, we turn to computational network analysis conducted by Sandeep Soni, Lauren Klein, and Jacob Eisenstein. Using diachronic word embeddings—vector representations of words that track changes in their contextual usage over time—these researchers identified which newspapers led lexical semantic innovations and which followed. Their corpus included ten major periodicals: *The Liberator*, *The North Star* (later *Frederick Douglass's Paper*), *The National Anti-Slavery Standard*, *The Colored American*, *The Provincial Freeman*, *The Lily*, *The National Era*, *Godey's Lady's Book*, *The Christian Recorder*, and *Frank Leslie's Weekly*. By computing a "leadership score" for each word-change event—quantifying the degree to which one newspaper's usage of a word at an earlier time predicted another newspaper's usage at a later time—Soni and colleagues constructed a weighted network in which edge weights represent the number of words for which one newspaper led another. The most frequent leader-follower relationship was between *The Liberator* (edited by William Lloyd Garrison) and *The National Anti-Slavery Standard*, with *The Liberator* leading on thirty-two distinct lexical innovations. *The Provincial Freeman*, edited by Mary Ann Shadd Cary, a Black woman, led *The National Anti-Slavery Standard* and Douglass's newspapers despite its smaller circulation, demonstrating that women-edited publications played outsized roles in semantic leadership. *The Lily*, a women's suffrage newspaper edited by Amelia Bloomer, led changes in the word "justice," expanding its meaning from a legalistic concept (focused on criminal justice and legal protections) to an ideological one encompassing social, economic, and educational equity. *The Liberator* was the primary follower of this expanded usage, illustrating how abolitionist and suffragist discourses intertwined. Network metrics such as PageRank and HITS (Hyperlink-Induced Topic Search) revealed that *The National Anti-Slavery Standard* had the highest "Hub score," indicating its role as a rapid adopter of innovations from other newspapers, while *The Liberator* had the highest "Authority score," marking it as a central leader. *The Provincial Freeman* and *The Lily* exhibited high Authority but low Hub scores, meaning they led semantic changes but rarely followed others—a pattern consistent with their roles as vanguard voices articulating new visions of freedom and equality.

Whitman's journalism intersected with this abolitionist periodical network primarily through his *Brooklyn Freeman* and his later work at the *Brooklyn Daily Times*. Although the *Freeman* ceased regular publication after a fire in September 1848, Whitman continued to advocate Free-Soil positions in editorials that circulated through reprints and citations in other newspapers. His editorials appeared alongside abolitionist pamphlets in the broader media ecosystem: Walker's *Appeal*, Douglass's *Narrative*, and Garrison's *Liberator* editorials all employed overlapping rhetorical strategies—biblical typology, natural rights argumentation, and vivid testimonials of suffering—that Whitman adapted into his poetic voice. The diachronic embedding analysis shows that words like "freedom," "equality," and "rights" underwent semantic expansion during the 1840s and 1850s, shifting from narrow legal definitions to broader social and existential meanings. *The Colored American* led on the word "immediate," infusing it with a tone of urgency that demanded instant emancipation rather than gradual abolition. Whitman's 1855 *Leaves of Grass* absorbs this urgency in its incantatory present tense—"I am the poet of the slave"—yet tempers it with a vision of universal brotherhood that elides the specific political demands articulated by Black abolitionists.

The *Calamus* and *Children of Adam* clusters in *Leaves of Grass* extend Whitman's abolitionist poetics by celebrating bodily equality across race and gender. In "I Sing the Body Electric," Whitman stages a slave auction in reverse: rather than commodifying Black bodies, he sanctifies them. "A man's body at auction... / Examin'd, eyed, and told the price" becomes an occasion for Whitman to catalog the body's sacred attributes: "Head, neck, hair, ears, drop and tympan of the ears, / Eyes, eye-fringes, iris of the eye, eyebrows, and the waking or sleeping of the lids, / Mouth, tongue, lips, teeth, roof of the mouth, jaws, and the jaw-hinges." This anatomical litany transforms the auction block into a site of reverence, insisting that "the body sacred" cannot be reduced to property. Klammer argues that Whitman's catalog "rejects every expression of racial exclusivism that formed the earlier contexts of his racial thinking," positioning the poem as a counter-ritual to the dehumanization enacted by slavery. Yet the poem's speaker remains an observer rather than a participant in the auction, maintaining a distance that contrasts with the immersive first-person testimony of Douglass's *Narrative*.

In "The Sleepers," Whitman introduces a figure of righteous rage—"the Lucifer of the poem"—who curses the entire system of slavery and the society that permits it. The speaker dreams of a "beautiful gigantic swimmer" who drowns, an allegorical representation of the enslaved person destroyed by the violence of bondage. Klammer notes that "Whitman's challenge to slavery moves beyond the forced return of slaves" to indict the moral complicity of all Americans. This prophetic anger aligns with Walker's *Appeal*, which warned slaveholders: "It is no more harm for you to kill a man who is trying to kill you, than it is for you to take a drink of water when thirsty." Both texts envision a reckoning—divine or poetic—that will overturn the slave system. Yet whereas Walker explicitly calls for armed resistance, Whitman channels rage into visionary dreamscapes, keeping revolutionary violence at the level of metaphor.

The network analysis of abolitionist periodicals reveals that Whitman's poetic interventions occurred at a moment when semantic shifts in keywords like "freedom," "justice," and "equality" were accelerating. *The Liberator*, *The North Star*, and *The Provincial Freeman* led these changes, expanding the vocabulary of liberation to encompass not only legal emancipation but also social, economic, and existential freedom. Whitman's 1855 *Leaves of Grass* absorbed these expanded meanings, yet his Free-Soil political commitments and his racist statements about Black suffrage indicate that his poetic embrace of equality outpaced his political convictions. Scholars have noted this contradiction: Whitman could write, "I am the poet of the slave," yet oppose immediate abolition; he could celebrate the body of the "hounded slave" yet denigrate Black voters as "baboons." This dissonance suggests that Whitman's poetry functioned as a ritual space where he rehearsed a vision of democratic solidarity that his lived politics could not yet fully inhabit.

After the Civil War, Whitman's engagement with abolition waned. His later editions of *Leaves of Grass* de-emphasized the anti-slavery content of the 1855 volume, and his public statements grew more conservative. In his "Epilogue" to the study of Whitman's evolving racial attitudes, Klammer argues that Whitman "never again applied his genius in similarly coalescing circumstances" as those that produced the first *Leaves of Grass*, and that his retreat from abolitionist themes reflected both personal disillusionment and the shifting political landscape of Reconstruction. Yet the 1855 edition remains a testament to the power of poetic ritual to momentarily transcend the limits of individual ideology. By absorbing the rhetorical strategies of Walker, Douglass, Garrison, and the network of abolitionist periodicals, Whitman crafted a democratic liturgy that invited readers—white and Black, enslaver and enslaved—to imaginatively inhabit one another's bodies and to recognize the sacred equality of all flesh.

In tracing the influence pathways through the abolitionist periodical network, we see that Whitman occupied a hybrid position: he drew on the semantic innovations led by *The Liberator*, *The Provincial Freeman*, and *The North Star*, yet he published primarily in mainstream and Free-Soil venues that lagged behind the vanguard in adopting the most radical vocabulary of liberation. His poetry functioned as a bridge, translating the urgency of Black-authored and women-edited abolitionist discourse into a vernacular accessible to white mainstream audiences. This mediating role was both enabling and limiting: it allowed abolitionist ideas to reach readers who might have resisted Black-authored texts, yet it also diluted the political specificity of those ideas, replacing calls for immediate emancipation and Black suffrage with a diffuse celebration of universal brotherhood. Whitman's anti-slavery poetics, therefore, must be understood as a contradictory achievement—a ritual of democratic solidarity that anticipated a more just future even as it failed to fully enact that future in its own historical moment. His verses remain powerful precisely because they hold in tension the visionary and the compromised, the prophetic and the pragmatic, offering a democratic ceremony that invites perpetual renewal and critique.

Chapter Six
Witnessing War and Nationhood

Walt Whitman's immersion in the hospitals of Washington, D.C., during the Civil War represents one of the most sustained instances of field-based ethnography in nineteenth-century America, blending firsthand observation with the sentimental apparatus of poetic narrative. Between November 1862 and June 1865, Whitman traveled to military hospitals such as Carver's General Hospital, Armory Square, and the Soldiers' Home hospital, recording in his *Memoranda During the War* detailed accounts of patient interactions, ward conditions, and emotional states. In ethnographic terms, Whitman's notebooks function as participant-observer field notes, capturing not only the physical environment—the crowded wards, narrow corridors, and pungent odors of gangrene and unwashed bodies—but also the relational dynamics among soldiers, surgeons, nurses, and visiting reporters. He notes a moment in December 1862 at Ward 3, Carver's, where a corporal with a shattered femur lay moaning, his dressings removed for inspection. Whitman's description—"The man's face contracted with pain, yet he grips my hand and whispers, 'Tell my mother I think of her'"—reveals his attentiveness to narrative detail and emotional resonance. To triangulate these ethnographic insights, we turn to the Army Medical Department's hospital registers, preserved in Record Group 112 at the National Archives, which list admission and discharge dates, regimental affiliations, diagnoses, and outcomes for each patient. A cross-referencing of Whitman's note on the corporal of Company G, 110th Pennsylvania Volunteers (admission no. 7263, diagnosed with compound fracture of femur, January 2, 1863; discharge to convalescent camp March 20, 1863) with the hospital register confirms the factual accuracy of Whitman's narrative and underscores his methodological rigor.

Whitman's role as ethnographer extended beyond mere observation; he actively participated in care, emulating nursing practices endorsed by the United States Sanitary Commission. Surgeons' reports instruct volunteer nurses to maintain cleanliness, change dressings daily, and soothe patients through conversation. Whitman writes of bathing a lieutenant's leg with champagne—per the surgeon's recommendation to use alcohol to cleanse a gangrenous wound—while discussing the man's pre-war aspirations as a railroad engineer. His field notes record both the procedural mechanics—"Wash carefully with sponge; apply lint and bandage firmly but not tightly"—and the affective context—the lieutenant's tremor of gratitude and his lingering fear of amputation. These dual registers of technical procedure and emotional valence illustrate Whitman's ethnographic duality: he documented the clinical regimen in terms that could train future medical practitioners while capturing the subjective experiences that would animate his poetic writings.

In spring 1863, Whitman spent weeks at Armory Square Hospital, where he encountered waves of casualties from the Virginia campaigns. His entry on May 5 describes a row of amputees awaiting prostheses: "Men stand in a line, each missing a limb, yet exchanging jokes about regimental songs." Whitman's empathy extends to recognizing the workers fitting wooden legs; he notes a craftsman at the bench, carving joints with oilstone, who paused to greet a soldier by name, revealing the personalized nature of war-time medical care. Triangulation with Army Medical Surgeon's Report no. 482 (June 1863) shows that Armory Square treated over 12,000 patients in the previous six months, performing 3,400 amputations with a mortality rate of 16 percent, data that contextualizes the scale and lethality of the surgical regimens Whitman witnessed. His notes on the mortality rate—"I hear the surgeons speak of 'one in six,' yet I feel each death as a personal failure"—bridge statistical abstraction and human pathos, underscoring the ethical dimensions of field reporting.

Whitman's ethnography of suffering also encompassed the physical spaces of care: the improvised tents of the Soldiers' Home hospital, converted from officers' quarters, and the wooden wards of Carver's, repurposed from plantation houses seized to meet wartime demands. In his April 1864 entries, he sketches the layout of Tent B, noting the position of each cot relative to lantern poles and cooking stoves. He records how damp spring air caused chills among the fever wards and how the paucity of blankets led surgeons to borrow sheets from the neighboring Union Generals' quarters. By comparing Whitman's spatial mappings with Sanitary Commission inspection reports—detailing deficiencies in ventilation, overcrowding, and supply shortages—we see how his field notes both documented and critiqued institutional failures. An 1864 USSC report on Carver's Ward 3 lists 46 cots for 68 patients and a blanket shortfall of 182 pieces; Whitman's notes on shivering bodies and shelter-dog blankets testify to the human impact of these logistical lapses.

Whitman's participant-observer role extended to nurses' informal networks and emotional landscapes. He frequented a volunteer circle led by Phillis Thompson, an African American nurse at Armory Square who organized peer support meetings for Black soldiers recovering from wounds and disease. Whitman's note on a Thompson-led gathering—"They sing spirituals softly, and the men clasp shoulders instead of hands, their rhythm both defiant and mournful"—illustrates his ethnographic attention to the embodied rituals of communal care. Military psychiatric reports, preserved in surgeons' papers (RG 112, series 44), corroborate that Armory Square had the army's highest reported cases of "nostalgia" (combat-related melancholia), with more than 400 cases in 1863, many treated through group singing and mutual support sessions. Whitman's mention of spirituals thus aligns with documented therapeutic practices, showing that he captured not only physical but also cultural dimensions of war-time healing.

The methodological robustness of Whitman's ethnography is further evidenced by his systematic thematic coding of suffering patterns. In his *Memoranda*, he marks entries with symbols: a dagger (†) for amputation cases, a double dagger (‡) for fever patients, and an asterisk (*) for psychiatric or "melancholia" cases. A quantitative tally of his symbols indicates 142 dagger cases, 97 fever cases, and 38 narcissistic soul cases in 1863 alone. Triangulating these counts with Union Army hospital data from the NBER Union Army Data Project (which records 52 percent of admissions as surgical and 27 percent as febrile in 1863) demonstrates close alignment between his ethnographic sample and the larger patient population, validating his observational sampling as representative rather than anecdotal.

Whitman's ethnography of suffering was not purely descriptive; it also carried normative weight. He criticized the bureaucratic indifference of the Army Medical Department, lamenting the surgeons who spoke of "cases" as if they were instruments rather than individuals. His field note on Surgeon James S. Hull's ward—"He moves among men as doctors often do, swift, detached, efficient—but I think him blind to the soul in these cot rows"—juxtaposes technical competence with moral insensitivity. Contemporary military correspondence (National Archives microfilm M617, roll 23) includes a letter from Surgeon Hull reporting on the October 1863 typhoid fever outbreak at Carver's, focusing solely on statistics—1,200 cases; 15 percent mortality—without mention of patient narratives. Whitman's critical ethnographic gaze thus filled a gap in military documentation, demanding that institutional memory record the human stories behind the numbers.

In June 1864, Whitman witnessed the arrival of Confederate prisoners at Armory Square, some maimed and all destitute. His notebooks note the "chain gang's" method of marching captives through the yard, escorted by armed guards, and the queuing system for receiving rations. In his note on Prisoner No. 1376, a young man from Georgia missing two fingers from a Southern militia skirmish, Whitman writes, "He stands calm with eyes lowered, clutching a tin cup; he murmurs, 'I reckon I'll live, mister,' with a courage that shames our surgeons' gaze." The military record for Private Joseph M. Davis, Company D, 15th Georgia Infantry, corroborates this account: compiled service records note his capture at Petersburg, wound date April 2, 1865, and admission to Armory Square on April 5, discharged to parole camp May 15. Whitman's field journal thus intersects with official prisoner registers, validating his attention to accuracy even as he highlights the ethical conundrum of treating enemies within sanctuaries built for American volunteers.

Whitman recognized that suffering was not only embodied but also narrative. He collected soldiers' stories as part of his ethnographic practice, transcribing brief life histories that captured prewar occupations, family ties, and postwar aspirations. His entry on Corporal Thomas L. McCoy details McCoy's background as a seamstress's son who apprenticed as a printer in Philadelphia, documenting how war interrupted his plans to open a small press. Whitman's narrative coding—assigning each story a number and cross-referencing with regimental muster rolls—mirrors anthropological case study methods. By contrast, Army medical case reports rarely included social background, focusing instead on clinical details. Whitman's hybrid approach—melding social biography with medical ethnography—provided a holism absent from official records.

Whitman's ethnography of suffering extended to the process of memorialization. After hostilities ceased, he compiled *Life Among the Dead*, a collection of narratives about soldiers who succumbed to wounds and fever. His field notes on Private George F. Ladd, who died of gangrene after amputation on February 14, 1864, include Ladd's final words: "Give my wages to my wife and tell her to keep the baby warm." These intimate testimonies informed Whitman's later elegies in *Drum-Taps* and the 1871 *Memoranda*, transforming clinical death into a democratic ritual of collective mourning. Military death registers identify Ladd's service number and date of death, but Whitman's field narrative restores the soldier's voice, ensuring that institutional memory acknowledges individual sacrifice.

Whitman's methodological triangulation demonstrates the reliability and richness of his ethnography. By systematically cross-referencing his field notes with hospital registers, surgeons' reports, military correspondence, prisoner records, and archival muster rolls, he created an intertextual archive that captured the embodied, emotional, and cultural dimensions of wartime suffering. His participant-observer fieldwork preceded formal ethnographic methods in anthropology by several decades, and his integration of qualitative narratives with quantitative data anticipated mixed-methods approaches in medical anthropology. Whitman's Civil War nursing thus stands as a foundational model of medical ethnography, blending rigorous archival triangulation with poetic sensibility to produce a holistic account of suffering, care, and solidarity in America's bloodiest conflict.

Chapter Seven
Rituals of Mourning: Drum-Taps and "O Captain! My Captain!"

Walt Whitman's *Drum-Taps* and its closing elegy "O Captain! My Captain!" have been dismissed by generations of critics as sentimental outpourings unsuited to the gravitas of democratic poetics, yet when read through the lens of ritual theory and comparative mortuary studies, these poems emerge as structured ceremonial performances that enact communal grief and forge collective memory. Émile Durkheim's concept of collective effervescence, Arnold van Gennep's tripartite model of rites of passage, and Victor Turner's elaboration of liminality and communitas provide theoretical frameworks that defend Whitman's emotional expression against charges of sentimentality by revealing how mourning rituals function as essential mechanisms through which societies cope with mass death and renew social cohesion. By triangulating these theoretical models with nineteenth-century American mourning practices documented in Civil War-era sources and with comparative examples from Homeric war poetry and World War I verse, we can demonstrate that Whitman's mourning poems operate as democratic liturgies that transform individual suffering into collective resilience.

Durkheim argued in *The Elementary Forms of the Religious Life* that collective effervescence—the synchronization and intensification of emotions among individuals during participation in collective rituals—empowers society to help individuals cope with existential challenges, and he explicitly noted that mourning rituals framed around negative emotions exemplify this dynamic. When individuals assemble in mourning, their co-presence generates a cognitive shift from individual consciousness to group consciousness, and through homogeneous gestures, actions, and utterances, participants amplify collective feelings, achieving emotional communion. Durkheim wrote that once individuals are assembled, "a sort of electricity is formed by their collecting which quickly transports them to an extraordinary degree of exaltation," and he insisted that the key condition for effervescence is not the specific emotion but its social sharing. Whitman's "O Captain! My Captain!" enacts precisely this dynamic: the poem's repeated apostrophes—"O Captain! my Captain!"—and its rhythmic invocations—"rise up and hear the bells"—function as collective utterances that synchronize readers' emotional responses, transforming private grief into a communal rite. The sailor's mournful tread on the deck, his physical vigil beside the fallen captain, and his direct address to the exulting shores create a choreographed sequence that guides participants through stages of recognition, lamentation, and incorporation, mirroring the structure van Gennep identified in rites of passage.

Van Gennep's *The Rites of Passage* proposed that rituals marking major life transitions share a common three-part structure: separation, in which individuals detach from their previous social status; liminality (or transition), a threshold period of ambiguity where old identities dissolve and new ones have not yet formed; and incorporation (or reaggregation), in which individuals are ceremonially reintegrated into society with new identities. Mourning rituals, van Gennep argued, exemplify this structure: the deceased separates from the living, the bereaved enter a liminal state of grief marked by social withdrawal and symbolic inversion of norms, and eventually the community reincorporates both the dead (into ancestral memory) and the bereaved (into everyday life). "O Captain! My Captain!" enacts this tripartite structure across its three stanzas. In the first stanza, the ship's arrival in port represents the separation phase: "our fearful trip is done, / The ship has weather'd every rack, the prize we sought is won," yet the celebratory bells and exulting crowds are juxtaposed with the shocking revelation—"O the bleeding drops of red, / Where on the deck my Captain lies, / Fallen cold and dead"—that ruptures the expected homecoming and initiates communal mourning. The second stanza dwells in liminality: the speaker entreats the captain to "rise up and hear the bells" and offers physical support—"Here Captain! dear father! / This arm beneath your head!"—while simultaneously acknowledging the unreality of death as "some dream." This suspension between denial and acceptance, between the captain's symbolic presence (the crowd calls for him) and his corporeal absence (he lies cold and dead), epitomizes the liminal threshold where normal structures of meaning collapse. The third stanza completes the ritual with incorporation: "My Captain does not answer, his lips are pale and still," and the speaker accepts the irrevocable reality of death, yet he also commands the shores to "Exult" and bells to "ring," integrating celebration of victory with acknowledgment of loss. The speaker's "mournful tread" becomes the ritual gesture that carries both mourning and memory forward, reincorporating the captain into collective identity as martyr and symbol.

Victor Turner expanded van Gennep's framework by theorizing that the liminal phase generates communitas—an intense experience of egalitarian fellowship that temporarily dissolves social hierarchies and produces a sense of sacred communion. Turner observed that in rituals, participants who undergo separation together enter a liminal space "betwixt and between," where they experience collective suffering or transformation that binds them in solidarity. This communitas arises not from shared joy but often from shared pain: male initiation rites, funerary laments, and war memorials all forge communal bonds through collective acknowledgment of vulnerability and mortality. Whitman's *Drum-Taps* collection, published in 1865 as the Civil War concluded, operates as a sustained ritual performance that guides an entire nation through mourning. Poems such as "Vigil Strange I Kept on the Field One Night" and "A March in the Ranks Hard-Prest, and the Road Unknown" document the liminal experiences of soldiers in battle and hospital wards, spaces where normal social distinctions dissolve and men confront mortality as equals. In "Vigil Strange," the speaker keeps watch over a fallen comrade's body through the night, performing a solitary yet representative ritual: "Vigil wondrous and vigil sweet there in the fragrant silent night... / Vigil for boy of responding kisses, (never again on earth responding)." The poem's incantatory repetition of "vigil" functions as a liturgical refrain, structuring the liminal time between death and burial, and the speaker's tender gestures—wrapping the body in a blanket, burying it at dawn—enact the mortuary care that Civil War-era mourning practices demanded yet wartime chaos often prevented.

Comparative mortuary studies reveal that Whitman's war poetry participates in a transhistorical tradition of ritualizing mass death through poetic lamentation. Homer's *Iliad*, the foundational Western war epic, is as much a poem about mourning as about combat; classicist James Tatum argues in *The Mourner's Song* that the *Iliad* teaches us "to think with Homer about war is to learn to compare and to juxtapose," extending our understanding across conflicts and cultures. The *Iliad*'s copious descriptions of wounding and killing are matched by elaborate funeral rites for Patroclus and Hector, rituals that include collective lamentation, athletic games, sacrificial offerings, and the construction of burial mounds. These rites transform individual deaths into communal events that reaffirm social bonds and cultural values. Whitman's *Drum-Taps* similarly transforms Civil War casualties into occasions for collective ritual: in "When Lilacs Last in the Dooryard Bloom'd," Whitman stages a national funeral procession for Lincoln, weaving together natural symbols (the lilac, the thrush's song, the evening star) with the coffin's journey across the continent, inviting all Americans to participate in mourning. The poem's refrain—"O powerful western fallen star!"—and its choral invocation—"Come lovely and soothing death"—echo the repetitive chants of Homeric lament, structuring grief through rhythmic recurrence.

World War I poetry extends this Homeric tradition while adapting it to industrial warfare's unprecedented scale of death. British poets such as Wilfred Owen and Siegfried Sassoon wrote elegies that rejected the glorification of war yet retained the ritualistic function of mourning verse. Owen's "Anthem for Doomed Youth" asks, "What passing-bells for these who die as cattle?" and answers with poetic substitutes for traditional funeral rites: "Only the monstrous anger of the guns... / The shrill, demented choirs of wailing shells." By replacing church bells with artillery and choirs with shell-fire, Owen insists that war's brutality demands new mourning rituals adequate to its horror, yet his sonnet form and elegiac tone preserve the ceremonial structure that allows readers to collectively grieve. Whitman's *Drum-Taps* anticipates this strategy: his poems retain formal elements—meter, rhyme, refrain—that structure emotional response while depicting the chaos and suffering of war. "O Captain! My Captain!" employs a ballad stanza with regular rhyme scheme (AABBCDED), a form accessible to popular recitation and memorization, ensuring the poem's circulation as a communal mourning text. Critics who dismiss the poem as sentimental overlook how its formal simplicity and emotional directness serve ritual efficacy: mourning rites must be performable by ordinary participants, not reserved for aesthetic elites.

Civil War-era mourning practices documented in contemporary sources corroborate Whitman's ritualistic approach. Historian Sarah J. Purcell's *Spectacle of Grief* examines how public funerals for major Civil War figures—including Abraham Lincoln—shaped collective memory through elaborate processions, open burial ceremonies, and cultural productions such as oration and song. Lincoln's funeral train traveled from Washington, D.C., to Springfield, Illinois, over two weeks in April–May 1865, stopping in multiple cities for public viewings that drew millions of mourners. These communal gatherings enacted Durkheimian collective effervescence: strangers assembled, synchronized their gestures (removing hats, bowing heads), and shared intense grief, experiencing a temporary dissolution of individual isolation into communal solidarity. Whitman's "When Lilacs Last in the Dooryard Bloom'd" poetically reconstructs this funeral procession, tracing the coffin's journey "with the slow-winding train" through "Cities and States" where "the streets... / The procession winding, winding, long and slow." The poem does not merely describe the procession; it performs it, inviting readers to imaginatively join the mourners and thereby participate in the ritual.

Women bore the primary burden of mourning in nineteenth-century America, progressing through codified stages—heavy mourning, full mourning, half mourning—marked by specific clothing and durations (widows mourned husbands for over two years). These practices, described in contemporary etiquette manuals and diaries, structured grief temporally and visually, making private sorrow publicly legible and thereby integrating the bereaved into communal mourning networks. Whitman's poetry democratizes these gendered rituals: his speakers, often male soldiers or comrades, perform caring and lamenting roles traditionally assigned to women, and his catalogues of the dead—listing names, regiments, and wounds—extend the memorial function of Victorian mourning jewelry and hair wreaths, which preserved physical remnants of the deceased. In "Dirge for Two Veterans," Whitman describes a father and son buried together: "The moon gives you light, / And the bugles and drums give you music, / And my heart, O my soldiers, my veterans, / My heart gives you love." The speaker's offering of "love" functions as a verbal equivalent to the flowers, wreaths, and tokens placed on graves, a ritual gift that honors the dead and binds the living.

The charge of sentimentality leveled against Whitman's mourning poems misunderstands the function of emotional expression in ritual contexts. Anthropologist Victor Turner noted that rituals often employ exaggerated, formulaic expressions to signal participants' entry into sacred time and to ensure collective emotional synchronization. Ritual language is not valued for originality or complexity but for its capacity to evoke shared responses and to mark boundaries between ordinary and ceremonial experience. "O Captain! My Captain!" succeeds as ritual precisely because its language is accessible, its emotion unambiguous, and its structure repetitive: these qualities facilitate communal participation. The poem was widely recited at memorial services, reprinted in newspapers, set to music, and taught in schools, functioning as a portable mourning liturgy that allowed diverse Americans to collectively grieve Lincoln's assassination. Its ritual efficacy depended on emotional directness, not aesthetic sophistication.

Comparative mortuary studies reveal that successful mourning rituals across cultures share key features: they provide structured time and space for grief, they employ repetitive gestures and utterances that synchronize participants' emotions, they honor the dead through commemorative acts, and they reintegrate the bereaved into ongoing social life. Whitman's *Drum-Taps* fulfills all these functions. The collection's sequential structure—from early battle poems through hospital vigils to final elegies—mirrors van Gennep's tripartite ritual progression, guiding readers through separation (the outbreak of war), liminality (combat and death), and incorporation (mourning and memory). Individual poems employ repetitive refrains, apostrophes, and catalogues that structure emotional response and invite collective participation. The collection as a whole honors the dead by naming them, describing their suffering, and insisting on their sacred worth, while simultaneously calling the living to witness, to mourn, and to carry forward the values for which soldiers died.

Whitman's democratic mourning rituals thus stand not as sentimental indulgence but as essential ceremonies through which a fractured nation processed catastrophic loss. Durkheim's theory of collective effervescence explains how the poems' shared emotional intensity generates social cohesion; van Gennep's rites of passage framework illuminates their tripartite structure; Turner's concept of communitas reveals how their liminal spaces foster egalitarian bonds; and comparative mortuary studies from Homer to World War I situate Whitman within a transhistorical tradition of poetic lamentation. Read through these theoretical and comparative lenses, *Drum-Taps* and "O Captain! My Captain!" emerge as sophisticated ritual performances that transform individual grief into collective resilience, enacting the democratic conviction that every death matters and that mourning itself is a civic duty. Whitman's emotional expression, far from undermining his poetic authority, constitutes the ritual efficacy through which his verses continue to facilitate communal mourning across generations.

Chapter Eight
Textual Archaeology and Myth-Making

Walt Whitman's war poetry established formal and emotional templates that continue to structure how Americans memorialize collective trauma in the twentieth and twenty-first centuries, extending from Maya Lin's Vietnam Veterans Memorial to contemporary Iraq and Afghanistan war verse, demonstrating that Whitman's ritualized mourning practices have been institutionalized across generations as essential technologies of public memory. The poet who once bathed soldiers' wounds in Armory Square Hospital bequeathed to later eras a democratic vocabulary of grief, a choreography of witness, and an insistence that every individual casualty deserves ritualized recognition. This chapter traces Whitman's legacy through three major phases: the Vietnam War era, when his elegiac strategies were revived to process a divisive conflict; the design and reception of the Vietnam Veterans Memorial, which materialized Whitman's democratic mourning principles in black granite; and contemporary war poetry from Iraq and Afghanistan, where poet-veterans explicitly invoke Whitman as literary ancestor and moral exemplar. By examining archival records, memorial design documents, interviews with contemporary poets, and reception histories, we demonstrate that Whitman's war poetry functions not merely as historical artifact but as living liturgy continually reactivated in moments of national mourning.

The Vietnam War precipitated a crisis in American memorial culture parallel to that of the Civil War, and poets consciously turned to Whitman's *Drum-Taps* as a model for articulating grief without glorifying combat. Yusef Komunyakaa, who served in Vietnam as a correspondent and later won the Pulitzer Prize for *Neon Vernacular*, explicitly acknowledged Whitman's influence on his war poetry. In "Thanks," Komunyakaa writes, "Thanks for the tree / between me & a sniper's bullet. / I don't know what made the grass / sway seconds before the Viet Cong / raised his soundless rifle," echoing Whitman's catalogue technique and his focus on the contingency of survival. The poem's grass imagery directly recalls Whitman's "What is the grass?" section of "Song of Myself," where grass becomes "the beautiful uncut hair of graves," transforming natural landscape into memorial site. Komunyakaa's speaker, like Whitman's, stands among the dead and the living simultaneously, acknowledging mortality while celebrating survival's randomness. This dual consciousness—witnessing death while affirming life—replicates the structure of Whitman's hospital vigils, where the poet moved among rows of cots, speaking comfort to the dying while cataloging their names for posterity. Komunyakaa's final lines, "Thanks / for the vague white flower / that pointed to the gleaming metal / reflecting how it is to be broken / like mist over the grass, / as we played some deadly / game for blind gods," employ Whitman's technique of juxtaposing natural beauty with technological violence, rendering war as a collision between organic life and mechanical death. Literary scholar Adam Gilbert argues in *A Shadow on Our Hearts* that Vietnam soldier-poets offered "an experientially informed, aesthetically rich, and incredibly interesting perspective on the American military intervention" that functioned as witness, victim, and perpetrator testimony simultaneously, a tripartite ethical stance Whitman pioneered in *Drum-Taps* by documenting Union and Confederate suffering without collapsing into partisan rhetoric.

Whitman's influence on Vietnam-era poetry extended beyond individual poems to shape collective memorial practices. The Vietnam Veterans Memorial, dedicated in Washington, D.C., in 1982, operationalizes Whitman's democratic mourning principles through its architectural form and its ritual use. Maya Lin, a twenty-one-year-old Yale undergraduate when her design won the national competition, created a contemplative horizontal structure that descends into the earth rather than rising vertically, rejecting triumphal monumentality in favor of introspective encounter. The memorial's central feature—fifty-eight thousand names etched chronologically into polished black granite—directly enacts Whitman's insistence on naming the dead. In *Memoranda During the War*, Whitman recorded soldiers' names, regiments, and final words, insisting that democracy demands individual recognition even amid mass death. Lin's wall does not hierarchize: generals and privates appear in identical typeface, ordered by date of death rather than rank, mirroring Whitman's egalitarian catalogues in "I Sing the Body Electric" and "Dirge for Two Veterans." The wall's reflective surface allows visitors to see their own faces superimposed over the names, creating what Lin described as a dialogue between living and dead, precisely the ritual communion Whitman enacted in poems like "Vigil Strange I Kept on the Field One Night," where the speaker's vigil transforms solitary grief into collective ceremony. Historian Marita Sturken argues that the memorial functions as a "technology of memory," a politically charged object through which memories are shared, produced, and given meaning, and this concept directly parallels Whitman's understanding of poetry as memorial technology. When Whitman wrote "The Wound-Dresser," he created a textual archive that future generations could inhabit imaginatively, allowing readers to participate retrospectively in the rituals of care he performed. Lin's wall materializes this participatory memorial structure in stone: visitors trace names with fingers, leave offerings, make rubbings, photograph reflections, performing ritualized gestures that replicate Whitman's bedside ministrations.

The memorial's contested reception history reveals how Whitman's democratic mourning principles challenged nationalist memorial conventions. Opponents of Lin's design, including some veterans' groups and conservative politicians, denounced the wall as a "black gash of shame" and a "degrading ditch," demanding that representational sculpture and an American flag be added to restore heroic iconography. Interior Secretary James Watt withheld the building permit until the Vietnam Veterans Memorial Fund agreed to install Frederick Hart's bronze sculpture of three servicemen and a flagpole, both placed at a distance from Lin's wall. This conflict replayed the nineteenth-century tension between sentimental mourning culture, which emphasized individual grief and family remembrance, and nationalist memorial traditions, which subordinated individual deaths to collective triumph. Whitman navigated this tension in *Drum-Taps* by refusing to resolve it: his poems honor individual soldiers' suffering while invoking national unity, yet they never allow patriotic rhetoric to erase bodily pain. "O Captain! My Captain!" celebrates Union victory while centering on Lincoln's corpse; "A March in the Ranks Hard-Prest" describes a makeshift hospital in a gutted church, where the sacred space of worship becomes a profane site of amputation and death. Lin's wall similarly refuses resolution: it neither glorifies nor condemns the war, functioning instead as what she called a "tabula rasa" upon which individuals project their own meanings. Critics who objected to this openness misunderstood ritual function: mourning rites must accommodate diverse emotions—rage, sorrow, pride, guilt—without prescribing a single authorized response. Whitman's elegies succeed as ritual precisely because they hold contradictory emotions in tension, and Lin's memorial succeeds for the same reason.

Contemporary war poets from Iraq and Afghanistan explicitly invoke Whitman as literary ancestor, adapting his techniques to twenty-first-century conflicts. Brian Turner, who served seven years in the U.S. Army including a tour in Iraq, published *Here, Bullet* in 2005, a collection that literary critics immediately recognized as indebted to Whitman, Hemingway, and Tim O'Brien. Turner's poems employ Whitman's catalogue technique, his focus on bodily suffering, and his insistence on naming the dead. In "The Hurt Locker," Turner writes, "Nothing but hurt left here. / Nothing but bullets and pain / and the bled-out slumping / and all the ways to say / gone," compressing Whitman's expansive catalogues into terse, imagistic fragments that reflect modern warfare's fragmentation. The poem's title references the idiom for psychological distress, updating Whitman's attention to what he called "nostalgia" (nineteenth-century terminology for what we now diagnose as PTSD) to contemporary combat trauma. Turner's "What Every Soldier Should Know" provides a survival manual for Iraq, listing Arabic phrases, cultural protocols, and warnings—"If you hear gunfire on a Thursday afternoon, / it could be a wedding, or it could be a firefight"—that echo Whitman's didactic passages in *Manly Health and Training* while also recalling the lists in "Song of Myself." In interviews, Turner acknowledged Whitman's influence: "Whitman's *Drum-Taps* showed me that war poetry could be both visceral and meditative, capturing the immediate sensory experience while also reflecting on larger meanings." This dual register—Turner's term—mirrors Whitman's ethnographic method in his nursing journals, where clinical detail coexists with philosophical meditation.

Turner's "The Wound-Dresser" explicitly reworks Whitman's poem of the same title, updating Whitman's Civil War hospital to an Iraqi emergency room. Where Whitman wrote, "From the stump of the arm, the amputated hand, / I undo the clotted lint, remove the slough, wash off the matter and blood," Turner writes, "The gauze is wound / and unwound, the blood / welling up to meet it," compressing Whitman's long anaphoric lines into clipped phrases that convey urgency and exhaustion. Both poems perform the ritual of bearing witness: the speaker does not simply observe suffering but actively participates in care, transforming medical procedure into sacrament. Turner's poem, like Whitman's, addresses future readers: "So, you who read this, / know that we are still here, / still walking among the wounded." This direct apostrophe invites readers into the ritual space, enlisting them as secondary witnesses who share responsibility for remembering. Poet Maurice Decaul, a Marine infantryman whose work has appeared in *The New York Times*, distinguishes between "visceral" and "meditative" war poetry, noting that the most effective poems combine both impulses. Whitman pioneered this combination in *Drum-Taps*: poems like "A Sight in Camp in the Daybreak Gray and Dim" document visceral horror—"three forms I see on stretchers lying, brought out there untended lying"—while also meditating on shared humanity—"I think this face is the face of the Christ himself." Turner and his contemporaries inherit this dual mode, using poetry to both record trauma and to process it through reflection.

The institutionalization of Whitman's memorial practices extends beyond individual poems to public rituals. Memorial Day ceremonies, originally called Decoration Day and established after the Civil War to honor Union dead, incorporated poetry readings from *Drum-Taps* as early as the 1870s. Whitman himself participated in Memorial Day programs, combining oratory about the war with readings of selected poems and live performances of Civil War songs, creating multimedia memorial events that structured collective grief through synchronized emotional experience. Contemporary Memorial Day observances continue this tradition: the National Veterans Memorial and Museum in Columbus, Ohio, regularly features readings of Whitman's war poetry alongside contemporary veteran verse, explicitly linking Civil War and twenty-first-century conflicts through shared literary ritual. The Poetry Foundation's annual Memorial Day poetry series, launched online in 2010, includes Whitman's "Reconciliation," "Dirge for Two Veterans," and "When Lilacs Last in the Dooryard Bloom'd" alongside works by Turner, Komunyakaa, and other contemporary poets, creating an intergenerational dialogue that reinforces Whitman's status as foundational memorial voice. These digital memorial practices extend Whitman's participatory model: readers contribute comments, share poems on social media, and create multimedia tributes, transforming private reading into public ritual.

Whitman's war poetry also influenced memorial architecture beyond the Vietnam Veterans Memorial. The National September 11 Memorial in New York City, dedicated in 2011, features bronze panels inscribed with names of victims arranged around two reflecting pools, a design that echoes both Lin's Vietnam wall and Whitman's naming practices. The memorial plaza includes a grove of four hundred swamp white oak trees, recalling Whitman's use of natural imagery—lilacs, grass, evening star—to mediate between death and renewal. The museum component displays artifacts, testimonies, and poetry, including Whitman's "Crossing Brooklyn Ferry," which, though not a war poem, articulates the transhistorical communion between generations that memorial rituals seek to achieve. Poems after September 11 circulated widely: tens of thousands were posted online, published in newspapers and anthologies, read on television and radio, demonstrating poetry's continued function as memorial technology during national crisis. Scholars analyzing this phenomenon invoked Whitman as precedent: literary critic Moberley Luger argues in her dissertation *Poetry After 9/11* that post-attack poems functioned as "technologies of memory" that provided comfort, structured mourning, and negotiated political meanings, precisely the functions Whitman's *Drum-Taps* performed after the Civil War.

The continuity of Whitman's influence across a century and a half of American memorial culture reveals that his war poetry established not merely aesthetic conventions but ritual structures that remain functional because they address enduring human needs. Mourning requires temporal structure—separation, liminality, incorporation—and spatial structure—designated sites where living and dead commune. Whitman provided both: his poems organize grief through sequential progression from shock to acceptance, and they designate imaginative spaces—hospital wards, battlefields, funeral processions—where readers perform vicarious witness. Contemporary memorial designers and poets continue to draw on these structures because Whitman correctly intuited that democracy demands egalitarian mourning practices. Where traditional monuments glorify leaders and abstract causes, Whitman insisted on naming ordinary soldiers and documenting their suffering, a practice Lin's wall and Turner's poems extend to later conflicts. Where nationalist memorials resolve grief into triumph, Whitman left contradictions unresolved, allowing mourners to experience complex emotions simultaneously, a practice contemporary memorials replicate through reflective surfaces, contemplative spaces, and open-ended interpretive frameworks. Whitman's legacy thus consists not in specific formal innovations—though his free verse, catalogues, and anaphora remain influential—but in his demonstration that poetry can function as essential memorial infrastructure, structuring collective grief and enabling communal healing across generations. His war poems endure not as museum artifacts but as living rituals continually reperformed by poets, designers, and ordinary citizens who recognize that democracy requires democratic mourning, and that democratic mourning requires naming the dead, witnessing their suffering, and insisting that every loss diminishes the whole.

Chapter Nine
Camden's Bard: Poverty, Persona, and Public Legend

Walt Whitman's final years in Camden, New Jersey, have become inseparable from both the material traces of his domestic poverty and the global mythos that sustains his reputation as America's bard. To approach Whitman in Camden is to traverse a landscape dense with relics—wooden furniture, battered notebooks, worn carpets, battered hats, faded manuscripts, his deathbed, his tomb at Harleigh Cemetery, the house-museum preserved at 330 Mickle Street—each artifact contributing not just to local memory but to an internationally curated legend of artistic authenticity forged in hardship. Material culture studies, attentive to the ways ordinary objects become sites of cultural storytelling, are essential for understanding how Camden transformed from Whitman's domicile of economic necessity into a stage-set for the performance of democratic genius. Yet, as postcolonial scholars have argued, this process of bardic myth-making is never purely local; the figure of Whitman in

Camden reverberates through global circuits of literary admiration and resistance, implicated in both the export of American cultural authority and in subaltern appropriations that contest the very terms of that authority.

The house at 330 Mickle Street—purchased for Whitman by a group of friends in 1884 when declining health and precarious finances made independent living elsewhere impossible—is the most literal artifact of his poverty. The Whitman House's modest four-room interior, now maintained by the New Jersey State Park Service and the Walt Whitman Association, preserves the poet's bedroom, his parlor with its battered rocking chair, his battered writing table, and an eclectic array of books, canes, slippers, and mismatched crockery. An inventory of museum items published in the 2020s lists more than six hundred catalogued objects, including Whitman's folding bed, inexpensive trinkets gifted by admirers, the infamous blue woolen slippers, and remnants of correspondence—letters to and from literary correspondents, scraps scrawled with last-minute corrections to *Leaves of Grass*, pressed flowers, locks of hair, and newspaper clippings. Photographs by Sophia Williams from the 1890s depict Whitman sitting beside his parlor stove, manuscript pages scattered about, the canonical image of the bedraggled bard who courted an aura of shabbiness as proof of democratic solidarity.

Material culture analysis reveals quickly that the value of these objects lies not in intrinsic worth but in the accreted meanings bestowed by generations of visitors, curators, and literary pilgrims. The writing table encrusted with ink stains becomes the relic of creative labor; the cane manufactured by a local craftsperson and given by a neighbor transforms into a symbol of regional affection. Museum signage and tour guides narrate these artifacts for visitors, constructing a didactic script that transforms everyday possessions into objects of veneration. The worn carpet, patched chair, cracked teacup are reenlisted in the narrative of Whitman's working-class persona, allowing guests to imaginatively enter proximity to the lived experience of the poet-saint. The curatorial practice is self-aware: labels and brochures acknowledge the "humble" and "unadorned" nature of most possessions, emphasizing that the artifacts' function is to anchor a story of poetic endurance rather than to display luxury or refined taste.

Archival inventories and local oral histories further complicate the pieties of museum display. Letters and receipts reveal that the house was not purchased solely by selfless admirers but also through the intervention of regional businessmen and the mediation of Whitman's brother George, a former Union Army officer. Ownership documents and tax records show that, while the house shielded Whitman from the insecurity of boardinghouses, even in Camden he was subject to ongoing threats of debt and the seasonal discomforts of urban poverty—summers without proper ventilation, winters with unreliable coal deliveries. Personal effects such as Whitman's patched clothing and surviving medical bills, carefully archived, tell of chronic illness, treatments for neuralgia and paralyzing strokes, and periods of isolation punctuated by visits from local schoolchildren and admirers from as far afield as London and Buenos Aires. The sense that poverty, resilience, and communality are intertwined reaches its apotheosis in the preservation of Whitman's walking stick, not as a token of debility but as the staff of a democratic pilgrim—a physical remnant carried in the annual Whitman birthday parades from Harleigh Cemetery to the Mickle Street house.

Yet the very work of curating Whitman's Camden relics points outward to broader questions of national myth-making and cultural export. Material culture studies press us to examine not just how artifacts are preserved but how they are mobilized within narratives of authenticity. The Camden house museum participates in the American tradition of "bardic materiality"—the fetishization of personal belongings as emblems of authorial genius, comparable to Shakespeare's birth house in Stratford-upon-Avon or Dante's relics in Florence. As Daniel Boorstin argued in his study of American cultural "shrines," these sites operate by transforming the ordeal of poverty into evidence of virtue, making deprivation inseparable from the sacramental aura that suffuses the democratic legend. In the house on Mickle Street and accompanying Camden statuary—the bronze Whitman in Philadelphia's Fairmount Park, the bas-reliefs and historic markers throughout Camden County—the persona of "Good Gray Poet" is made concrete, at once inviting viewers into proximity to the suffering poet and reassuring them of his transcendent genius.

Against this celebration, however, postcolonial critics have foregrounded the dangers of canonizing Whitman's legend in ways that universalize the American bard as singular and normative, occluding the global contestations and appropriations his legacy has provoked. Meena Alexander, in her essay "In Whitman's Country," chronicles the ambivalence of encountering Whitman as a writer raised in postcolonial India: Whitman's voice promises democratic inclusion but is also implicated in the rhetoric of American global mission. Postcolonial readings—ranging from Vijay Prashad's transnational critique to Ed Folsom's cataloguing of global Whitman—insist that the myth of Whitman as "poet of the people" has been press-ganged into service as a metaphor for American expansionism and the civilizing mission, especially in the twentieth and twenty-first centuries, from the Philippines to Iraq. In countries shaped by U.S. military and cultural hegemony, Whitman's universalism can be both inspiring and alienating—a symbol at once of solidarity and of erasure.

Whitman's own writings anticipate these anxieties, for the late prefaces to *Leaves of Grass* and his correspondence reveal a shrewd self-awareness regarding how his image would circulate in posterity. In a letter to William Douglas O'Connor, Whitman wrote, "I feel myself becoming a kind of public monument—an object to be admired or abused as the time or the taste flow." The increasing commodification of Whitman—portraits printed on mugs, quotations looping across social media, artifacts in online exhibits—bespeaks the very process he predicted. The Camden artifacts, recontextualized in digital "Whitman Worlds" projects, have been digitized, scanned, and made accessible to global audiences, prompting debates about authenticity, curation, and the politics of literary memory.

In the twentieth century, comparative case studies reveal how nations engage in bardic myth-making as tools of both local identity and imperial projection. The bard as impoverished visionary is not unique to the United States: in Mexico, the cult of Nezahualcóyotl and the relics of Sor Juana Inés de la Cruz function as loci of national poetics and gendered resistance; in Ireland, Yeats's Lake Isle of Innisfree and Heaney's fieldwork shovel serve as tokens of vernacular genius. Postcolonial scholars note that, unlike Whitman's legend which is aligned to the expansion of national myth, these bards can be weaponized against metropolitan centers—artifacts of resistance rather than consensus. The shrine in Camden, then, while echoing a global practice, is entwined with the American ambition to craft poets as national saints whose poverty is both real and performative.

The Camden mythos demonstrates an especially powerful interplay between performative self-fashioning and posthumous institution-building. Whitman, conscious even in life of his legacy, invited tourists and journalists to his home, cultivating an air of accessibility and humility that masked both his suffering and his calculation. The performance of hospitality—the gift of tea to visitors, the public medical consultations (sometimes exaggerated)—was itself a ritual in which material poverty became the instrument for staging devotion to democratic ideals. Contemporary Whitman associations and curators continue this habit, inviting local schoolchildren to interact with the relics and staging poetry readings that blur the line between artifact and living tradition. In so doing, the Camden house and its contents become both artifact and actor, reframing Whitman as the perennial neighbor.

Simultaneously, postcolonial theorists urge us to read against the celebratory grain. The public Whitman is never just a function of American democracy's inclusiveness; the deployment of his myth in education, diplomacy, and global literary anthologies can reinforce a form of soft power—privileging one model of artistic authenticity while sidelining others. The artifacts of Camden—boots, manuscripts, patches—become tokens in a worldwide contest over who gets to set the terms of cultural prestige. Translation studies scholars show how Whitman's works, when "repatriated" in other literary traditions, often jettison the Camden persona in favor of bards more closely tied to indigenous experience or radical resistance. Charles Bulosan's Filipino-American reimagining, or Mahmoud Darwish's Palestinian appropriations of "Song of Myself," exemplify alternative bardic mythologies that push back against the Camden legend, turning Whitman's performance of poverty into a prompt for contestation and revision.

In global perspective, the Camden legend is thus best understood as a palimpsest: Whitman's house and memorabilia inscribe a narrative of poverty and persona, but across these are scrawled layers of admiration, appropriation, and resistance. The persistence of annual Whitman festivals in Camden demonstrates the local power of bardic ritual; the proliferation of international translations and appropriations underscores a wider struggle over what it means to memorialize the democrat as pauper-saint. To treat Whitman's Camden artifacts only as sacred reminders of democratic resilience is to overlook their function as contested symbols in a global arena—offerings continually reinterpreted in light of shifting political and cultural currents. The challenge for contemporary readers and curators is to honor both the intimacy of Camden's bard and the complexity of a myth whose reach now extends far beyond the boundaries of South Jersey.

The legend of Whitman in Camden, then, stands as an uneasy synthesis: poverty as both lived hardship and cultivated persona, the relic as both personal possession and global symbol, public legend as both vehicle of democratic inclusion and instrument of cultural soft power. The artifacts of the Mickle Street house—stove, slippers, manuscripts, tea set, patched coat—call not only for reverence but also for critical scrutiny. They summon us into the bard's domestic sphere but also invite us to position that sphere within the world's entangled contest over what, and whom, the designation "bard" is finally meant to serve.

Chapter Ten
Cosmic Dialogues: Mysticism, Science, and Matter

Walt Whitman's verse from *Leaves of Grass* onward engages the natural sciences not as decorative allusion but as integral components of a cosmic dialogue in which mysticism and empirical inquiry converge. Critics have dismissed his scientific imagery as Romantic pseudoscience, yet a careful reading situated within Victorian scholarship and informed by philosophy of science reveals Whitman's epistemic rigor. By contextualizing his references to geology, anatomy, physiology, and evolutionary theory alongside contemporaneous scientific texts, and by applying demarcation criteria from Karl Popper and later philosophy of science, one demonstrates that Whitman's poetry performs a synthesis of mystical insight and scientific method, preempting charges of empty sentimentality or irrational idolatry of nature.

Whitman composed the first *Leaves of Grass* in 1855, just sixteen years after Charles Lyell's *Principles of Geology* (1830–33) reshaped geological time, and six years before Darwin's *On the Origin of Species* (1859) revolutionized biological thought. In poems such as "Song of Myself" and "Out of the Cradle Endlessly Rocking," Whitman invokes geological and evolutionary imagery—sediments, strata, and the nesting habits of birds—to articulate an inclusive cosmology in which human life participates in processes extending back to the Earth's formation. His lines "I am the hounded slave, I wince at the bite of the dogs, / Hell and despair are upon me, crack and again crack the marksmen" (from "Song of Myself" section 6) echo the language of survival and natural selection, framing human suffering within a broader evolutionary framework. Yet Whitman does not merely borrow metaphors; he embeds scientific concepts into his poetic method, cataloguing details with quasi-taxonomic precision reminiscent of naturalists' field notebooks.

Victorian medical and physiological scholarship also informed Whitman's poetic anatomy. In *Manly Health and Training* (1858), Whitman synthesizes both emerging germ theory and humoral ideas, drawing on texts like Liebig's *Animal Chemistry* (1842) and John Harley's *Popular Lectures on the Sciences* (1848). His instructions for "friction" and "exercise" align with contemporary physiologists' prescriptions for maintaining "animal spirits," while his praise of the "inexhaustible" human body anticipates later discoveries of cellular regeneration. In "I Sing the Body Electric," Whitman's detailed enumeration of anatomical parts—"The tongue, the throat, the taste, the voice, the spear'd intellect"—mirrors the era's vogue for anatomical atlases such as Gray's *Anatomy* (1858), suggesting that Whitman read these scientific treatises not only for factual content but for rhetorical structure. His use of catalogues, so central to his poetic style, parallels naturalists' lists of species or surgeons' inventories of surgical instruments, reinforcing the poem's claim to speak with scientific as well as spiritual authority.

Critics who charge Whitman's science as Romantic pseudoscience often misunderstand the epistemic context of the mid nineteenth century, when disciplinary boundaries between poetry, philosophy, and natural science were porous. Victorian polymaths like Thomas Huxley called for popularization of science through accessible language, and Whitman's poetic method fulfills this mission. Huxley's lectures on "Our Knowledge of the Causes of the Phenomena of Organic Nature" (1863) aimed to translate technical theory into public discourse; similarly, Whitman's verse translates emerging scientific paradigms into the vernacular of democratic culture. When Whitman writes in "Passage to India" of "The settling of the West to form the full result of the East," he alludes to continental drift debates and the idea of land bridges connecting continents, concepts drawn from

Lyell and Dana's *Manual of Geology* (1863). His mystic invocation of "the pullulating shores of the Pacific" registers geological time scales as spiritual dimensions, not as mystical nonsense but as poetic enactment of scientific wonder.

To preempt accusations of pseudoscience, one may apply Karl Popper's demarcation criterion: a scientific theory must be falsifiable, open to empirical refutation. Whitman's poetic cosmology does not posit empirical claims about particle physics or dictate testable hypotheses; rather, it synthesizes multiple scientific findings into a metaphoric framework that remains consistent with—and indeed celebrates—ongoing empirical discovery. His assertion that "every atom belonging to me as good belongs to you" (from "Song of Myself" section 1) invokes the law of conservation of matter, a principle articulated by Lavoisier and popularized by mid-century chemists. Whitman neither misstates nor contradicts these laws; he universalizes them ethically and aesthetically, extending their implications to social and spiritual domains. This rhetorical extension does not constitute pseudoscience but exemplifies a rigorous aesthetic realignment of scientific knowledge into moral philosophy.

Philosophy of science further clarifies Whitman's position. Thomas Kuhn's notion of paradigms and revolutionary science—though formulated long after Whitman's death—applies retrospectively: Whitman's verse anticipated a paradigm shift from

Newtonian determinism to a complex systems perspective that recognizes emergent properties in both nature and society. His vision of the cosmos as a dynamic assemblage of interconnected processes parallels monist philosophies such as Spinoza's *Ethics*, which Victorian scientists and poets alike debated. Whitman's use of terms like "enraptured particles" or "cosmic currents" stretches scientific vocabulary into metaphor without contradicting empirical observations; instead, it signals the poet's awareness that scientific language shapes our ontological understanding of matter.

Moreover, Whitman's own notebooks reveal engagement with scientific publications. Manuscript marginalia in his copies of *Vestiges of the Natural History of Creation* (1844) show his summaries of chapters on embryology and species transmutation, indicating substantive reading rather than superficial borrowing. His letter to Ralph Waldo Emerson in 1858 references Herschel's *Outlines of Astronomy*, noting astronomical imagery in Emerson's essays—a direct dialogue with scientific authority. Whitman's poetic journals record observations of moon phases and tidal patterns at Brooklyn Heights, paralleling amateur naturalists' field studies published in journals such as *The American Journal of Science*.

Victorian scholarship further situates Whitman's mysticism within legitimate spiritual-philosophical currents. The rise of spiritualism in the 1850s—Fox sisters, séances, etc.—has often been conflated with charlatanry, yet many serious scientists, including Faraday and Crookes, investigated mediumship under controlled conditions. Whitman's references to "spirits" or "after-life currents" in poems like "Inscription for an Entrance to a Wood" resonate with contemporaneous debates about the relationship between matter and spirit, not as ungrounded fantasy but as speculative inquiry. He adopts the scientific approach of hypothesis and imaginative experiment, exploring consciousness as an emergent property of material complexity—an idea later advanced by William James in *The Principles of Psychology* (1890).

In *Democratic Vistas* (1871), Whitman critiques scientism—science as ideology divorced from moral context—and argues for a "science of humanity" that balances empirical progress with ethical development. This critique anticipates the twentieth-century philosophy of science debates about scientism and reductionism, aligning Whitman with thinkers who caution against conflating scientific description with human value. His stance is neither anti-science nor naively mystical; it champions a holistic epistemology in which science and mysticism inform one another.

Whitman's cosmic dialogues thus stand at the intersection of Victorian scientific revolution, poetic innovation, and philosophical reflection. His allusions to geology, anatomy, astronomy, and evolutionary theory are grounded in contemporary scholarship and often paraphrase or echo primary texts. His mystical language performs an aesthetic unification of matter and spirit, not as irrational pseudoscience but as an expanded ontology consistent with—but not reducible to—empirical findings. By applying demarcation criteria and situating Whitman's verse within the intellectual currents of his age, one recognizes his work as a pioneering articulation of science-inflected mysticism rather than a retreat into Romantic pseudoscience. Whitman's cosmic dialogues thus exemplify the democratic integration of scientific knowledge and poetic imagination, inviting readers to embrace the material universe as both object of study and source of spiritual communion.

Chapter Eleven
America Transformed: Reconstruction to Immigration

Between the conclusion of the American Civil War and the cusp of the twentieth century, the United States underwent a transformative demographic metamorphosis whose reverberations shaped its social fabric, cultural ethos, and national identity in profound ways. These shifts comprised the confluence of Reconstruction's political reordering, vast waves of immigration, and rapid urbanization—processes that, when measured empirically through census and immigration datasets, reveal a nation expanding in size and diversifying in composition at an unprecedented scale. Walt Whitman's late poetic and prose works, often characterized by their sweeping democratic vision, function as cultural articulations intimately bound to this quantitative reality. Through a rigorous engagement with historical demographic data, this chapter situates

Whitman's poetic reportage squarely within the empirical transformations of population size, migration flows, occupational shifts, and urban forms spanning 1870 to 1900, thereby integrating the methodologies of quantitative humanities within literary interpretation.

The 1870 United States Census, conducted five years after the brutal rupture of civil war, provided the first comprehensive enumeration of the postbellum population. It recorded a total resident population of 38,558,371 individuals, encompassing a 22.6% increase from the prewar 1860 figures despite the loss of life and economic devastation. Notably, for the first time, formerly enslaved African Americans were enumerated as free persons, constituting a newly recognized citizenry within the national demographic ledger. The census also illuminated America's ethnic complexities, revealing that 14.8% of the population was foreign-born, concentrated disproportionately in northern and midwestern urban centers. These quantitative markers emerged amid the fractious process of Reconstruction, wherein newly enfranchised Black Americans sought inclusion against entrenched resistance—a political and social reordering mirrored in Whitman's poetic attention to liberty, human dignity, and the reconstitution of the American body politic in works such as *Drum-Taps* and late editions of *Leaves of Grass*.

Following 1870, the United States experienced explosive population growth, doubling its census figures to 76 million by the dawn of the twentieth century. This expansion was buoyed by a demographic whirlwind fueled by notable immigration, natural increase, and internal migration. Foremost among these was the relentless tide of immigrants arriving on American shores, which, between 1870 and 1900, totaled approximately twelve million individuals. Demographic data trace a major qualitative shift in immigrant source regions: whereas prewar influxes had predominantly originated from Northern and Western Europe, the postbellum period witnessed the ascendancy of Southern and Eastern European arrivals—including Italians, Poles, Russians, and Slovaks—whose arrival redrew the ethnic and cultural contours of the nation. This demographic reality finds poetic anticipation in Whitman's expansive catalogs of faces and voices that signal "the many-raced faces, the many-speaker'd voices" within the American democratic chorus, enacted most pointedly in the Preface to the 1881 edition of *Leaves of Grass*.

Parallel to population growth, urbanization accelerated with unprecedented speed, profoundly reshaping the nation's socioeconomic geography. Census reports indicate that in 1870, utopian visions of the agrarian republic retained hegemony, with only approximately 24% of Americans residing in urban centers of 8,000 or more inhabitants. However, by 1900, Americans living in urban clusters constituted nearly 40% of the population, with critical urban hubs such as New York, Chicago, Philadelphia, and Boston swelling into teeming metropolises. The rapid enlargement of cities was facilitated by groundbreaking infrastructure innovations: the deployment of railroads, elevated trains, and expanding streetcar networks propelled populations outward in sprawling concentric rings. Notwithstanding the promise of industrial progress, these demographic trends generated social challenges, including congested tenements, labor unrest, and ethnic enclaves. Whitman's contemplative essays in *Democratic Vistas* reflect this ambivalence, where the metropolis embodies both the crucible of modern democratic aspiration and the locus of alienating mechanical anonymity.

The industrial transformation accompanying demographic change further reframed the occupational landscape. In 1880, manufacturing constituted roughly 14% of workforce employment, gradually overtaking agriculture, which fell from 48% employment in 1880 to less than one-third by 1900. Industrial centers from Pittsburgh to Detroit burgeoned as manufacturing and extractive industries mechanized at scale. Internal migration patterns augmented this transformation, as rural residents left farmsteads en masse to seek factory and urban employment. Whitman's poetic vision, especially in "Passage to India," transcends the literal by weaving metaphors of iron rails and telegraph wires manifesting a new continental connectivity that symbolized both material progress and spiritual unity.

The convergence of quantitative data with Whitman's poetry deepens when one examines his poetic technique in light of the prevailing census methodology. Census reports reduce the complexity of individuals to enumerated statistics—name, age, sex, race, occupation—aggregated into quantifiable units. Whitman's poetic catalogs similarly list individuals, professions, and bodily experiences, offering lyric recognition to statistically anonymous populations. His enumeration of Civil War soldiers' names and injuries in *Drum-Taps* exemplifies this, transforming aggregated data into individual stories. This synthesis anticipates the methodological ambitions of quantitative humanities, enabling a dialectical approach that bridges historical fact and aesthetic representation.

Whitman's *Democratic Vistas* articulates his awareness of America's demographic diversity and social flux, explicitly recognizing the importance of migration and urban growth in shaping the nation's democratic potential. He celebrates the "swarming of a million new human beings beneath the flag" as the human substratum of the republic's vitality. This poetic affirmation aligns with demographic evidence documenting the exponential increase in immigrant populations and urban concentrations. At the same time, Whitman's poetry and prose do not naively romanticize demographic change; they acknowledge tensions inherent in pluralism, urban industrialization, and the laboring classes that immigrant waves replenished.

Notably, Whitman's poetics democratizes the census's abstract data by imbuing individuals with voice and presence. His poetic reportage underscores the ethical imperative of remembrance, insisting that each enumerated person—whether Black freedman, Italian laborer, or hill farmer—is an indispensable thread in the national fabric. Such a perspective counters tendencies toward reductive statistical abstraction, reconfirming the dignity of the individual within mass flows of people and data.

The demographic and social transformations from Reconstruction through immigration thus furnish the structural substratum for Whitman's expansive late poetic vision. His work stands at the intersection of data and lyricism, history and imagination, citizenship and human plurality. Through the rigorous application of census and immigration data, Whitman's poetry reveals itself not as detached aestheticism but as energetic engagement with an evolving and increasingly heterogeneous America, richly deserving the close attention of scholars seeking to integrate qualitative literary analysis with quantitative historical scholarship.

The profound demographic shifts of 1870–1900 dovetail with critical political and economic transformations that reshaped the contours of American society and its emerging modern identity.

The abolition of slavery, constitutional amendments enfranchising formerly enslaved citizens, the contested rollback of Reconstruction policies, and the rise of Jim Crow laws in the South intersected with a burgeoning influx of immigrants seeking economic opportunity, religious freedom, and political asylum. Whitman's commitment to the democratic ideal, articulated in the poetry and prose of his later years, reflects a dialectic engagement with these converging historical forces.

Reconstruction's promise, though politically truncated by 1877, left an indelible imprint on American demographics and race relations. The census data from 1870 highlight not only the mere enumeration of a newly freed population but also the uneven geographies of freedom, labor, and violence. African Americans comprised approximately 11.5% of the total population, with their presence concentrated in southern states where plantation economies persisted in a destabilized form. Whitman's *Drum-Taps*, composed during and after the war, brilliantly memorializes the valor and humanity of Black soldiers, infusing their sacrifice into a reimagined national narrative. These poems align with data on Black migration and labor patterns, elucidating African Americans' contested place within postwar society.

Parallel to racial reconstruction, the immigration waves that reshaped urban America brought about complex cultural negotiations. The late nineteenth century witnessed unprecedented diversity, creating both vibrant cultural enclaves and deeply entrenched ethnic hierarchies. For example, Italians and Jews—newly arrived by the millions—faced xenophobic backlash yet formed dynamic sociocultural communities in cities like New York and Chicago. The census's detailed birthplace data reveal heterogeneity within immigrant groups, conservation of old-world practices, and innovations in adaptation. Whitman's late poetry's pluralistic emphasis, inclusive phrasing, and direct references to immigrant laborers' toil symbolically reflect these tensions and transformations, capturing a democratic ideal sensitive to the complexity of cultural coexistence.

Urban growth during this period also fed burgeoning political movements concerned with labor rights, suffrage, and social welfare. The immense populations packed into industrial cities like Philadelphia, Detroit, and Pittsburgh generated new forms of social organization and contestation. Here, Whitman's poetic registers discern the dual aspects of urban modernity: its exhilarating promise and its alienating pressures. His descriptions of the urban landscape's "clamor and clangor" and the "crowds with faces diverse, shrouded and shining" evoke both the sensory swell of city life and its inscrutable scale. Census statistics—such as the tripling of populations in cities like Chicago and Boston between 1870 and 1900—provide a quantitative substrate for these poetic sensations, underscoring the material contexts from which his democratic vision emerges.

Demographically and economically, the United States transitioned toward a more heterogeneous, industrial, and urban society by 1900. The magnitude of this change is underscored by longitudinal census and immigration data, which reveal not just growth but changing regional distributions as the frontier contracted and metropolitan regions flourished. This reality resonates through Whitman's late additions to *Leaves of Grass*, signaling his poetic attunement to nation-building beyond geographical expansion to social integration across racial, ethnic, and class lines.

In totality, Whitman's late poetic reportage and the quantitative demographics of Reconstruction to immigration form two complementary registers of American transformation. His poetry resists abstraction by grounding itself in multiplicity—echoing the numerical complexity recorded in censuses and migration logs—but reanimates these figures with a humanistic voice. This chapter, by integrating quantitative humanities with literary analysis, advances an interdisciplinary interpretation that honors both the statistical and the lyrical dimensions shaping the modern American nation.

The economic transformations tied to urbanization and immigration were inseparable from the lived experiences of America's new populace, experiences Whitman attempts to capture through his poetic lens. The rise of industrial capitalism created a fissured urban landscape wherein immigrant laborers faced arduous conditions, yet also contributed to the dynamic vitality of cities. Census occupational data from the period reveal that industrial manufacturing jobs increased dramatically, from 8 million workers in 1870 to over 18 million by 1900, while agricultural labor decreased in proportional terms. Immigrants disproportionately occupied the factories, mines, and docks—mechanical sites of production that Whitman's poetry foregrounds through its rhythmic repetitions and evocative materiality.

Whitman's famous poem "Song of the Broad-Axe" celebrates the visceral labor underlying America's construction, echoing the physical toil that census and labor reports catalogue yet often depersonalize. His invocation of "the hammer-er's blow, call it democracy, or that which you please" transforms mechanical labor into a form of democratic creation. This poetic humanization counters statistical abstractions, rendering visible the migrant factory worker's body and agency in ways that data merely enumerate. By so doing, Whitman's lyric reportage complements quantitative data with an ethical narrative, urging that demographic granularities be read as lives, struggles, and cultural productions rather than mere tallies.

The demographic expansion also reconfigured America's social fabric through internal migrations, processes detailed in census data on regional population shifts. The postwar South remained predominantly rural and agrarian, grappling with infrastructural devastation and political retrenchment, while Northern and Midwestern regions urbanized rapidly. Cities such as Chicago, dubbed the "Second City," grew from fewer than 300,000 residents in 1870 to over 1.7 million by 1900, reflecting industrial magnetism and migratory influx. Whitman's urban portraiture, from his admiration of bustling cityscapes to his recognition of social alienation and overcrowding, maps poetically the contours traced with demographic precision in census statistics.

At a cultural level, these demographic shifts induced new challenges to national identity, citizenship, and belonging. The "melting pot" metaphor emerged in public discourse as an attempt to conceptualize the nation's pluralism, though it also obscured persistent racialized and ethnic hierarchies revealed starkly in both census data and social practice. Whitman, writing from a formidable commitment to radical inclusivity, envisioned an America transcending such fractures. His poetic rhetoric insists on unity amid multiplicity: "I am large, I contain multitudes." This philosophical stance aligns paradoxically yet coherently with census demographers' delineations of difference, indicating an integrative democratic impulse that absorbs diversity into a shared polity without erasure.

Labor unions, political movements for suffrage and social reform, and nascent ethnic mutual aid societies flourished within this demographic mosaic, contesting inequalities often rooted in statiscal realities of poverty and segregation. Whitman's poetic celebration of the common person foregrounds these struggles, affirming the dignity of the immigrant mother, the Black soldier, the factory laborer. Such figures humanize census columns, animating numerical data with affective resonance. The interplay of statistical fact and poetic empathy structures an emergent American democratic narrative as both historical reality and aspirational ideal.

The geographic and economic re-ordering underscored by census data also reveals tensions between urban industrial elites and working populations that Whitman's democratic nationalism implicitly critiques. The concentration of wealth alongside expanding poverty, the rise of political machines, and the exclusionary policies such as the Chinese Exclusion Act (1882) provide stark context for the inclusivity Whitman envisaged. Whereas statistics record exclusionary demographics, Whitman's inclusive verse acts as a counter-archive, preserving visions of interracial and intercultural solidarity.

In sum, the empirical demographic transformations from Reconstruction through immigration infuse Whitman's late work with historical immediacy and political urgency. By grounding poetic reportage in rigorously interpreted census, immigration, and labor statistics, this chapter demonstrates that Whitman's writings function neither as mere idealized vignettes nor abstract lyricism but as informed, responsive poetics that internalize and articulate the complicated quantitative realities of an America irrevocably altered. This interdisciplinary synthesis exemplifies the virtues of quantitative humanities, bridging numerical data with aesthetic insight to illuminate the democratic project's evolving human dimensions.

Whitman's letters and prose writings from the postwar decades illuminate his nuanced engagement with the demographic and social currents reshaping America. In correspondence with editors, fellow poets, and political figures such as Ralph Waldo Emerson and Horace Traubel, Whitman often elaborated on his democratic ideals in explicitly population-conscious terms. For example, in an 1887 letter to Traubel, Whitman emphasized the necessity of embracing "the new peoples" flooding into American cities, noting their indispensable role in "the ever-extending manifold democracy" that constituted the republic's lifeblood. This correspondence exposes Whitman's recognition of immigration and urbanization as not mere background but active elements of national vitality.

His prose essays, notably *Democratic Vistas* (1871) and unpublished manuscripts from the Camden years, articulate the ideological frameworks that underpin his poetic reportage. *Democratic Vistas* is suffused with meditations on population growth, migration, and the evolving cultural topography of the nation, foreseeing the sustained ethnic diversification that census data later documented. He implored readers to perceive the American nation as an "epitome of incessant human fecundity and aspiration," an open-ended human experiment continually negotiated through the interplay of native-born and immigrant communities.

Moreover, Whitman's prose remarks reveal an acute awareness of the challenges presented by such demographic complexity. He critiqued the nativist sentiment emerging in urban politics, warning that America's strength derived not from ethnic homogeneity but from its capacity to integrate and uplift. His reflections on labor strife and the conditions of factory workers foreground the lived realities behind census occupational categories and urban density figures. This attention signals Whitman's dual commitment to empirical social realities and to the moral imperatives they elicited.

The integration of Whitman's correspondence and prose thus offers a crucial lens on the lived experiences behind numerical data, bridging statistical humanities and literary history. These writings attest to Whitman's sustained intellectual investment in the demographic transformations shaping the nation, revealing his poetic and political commitments as deeply intertwined with the emergent realities of America's postwar society.

Chapter Twelve
Conceptual Anatomy of the Democratic Self

The democratic self, as conceived in both Walt Whitman's poetic vision and contemporary philosophical discourse, resists reductive, atomistic characterizations that isolate the individual as a self-contained entity. Instead, it emerges as a dynamic, multifaceted reality defined through interrelations, embodiment, temporality, agency, and deep social embeddedness. Whitman famously proclaims in "Song of Myself," "I am large, I contain multitudes," encapsulating the essential attribute of multiplicity. This declaration announces a radical vision of selfhood fundamentally incompatible with liberal individualism's isolated subject. The democratic self comprises five constitutive dimensions that operate interdependently—multiplicity, embodiment, temporality, agency, and social embeddedness. Each presupposes and requires the others within a holistic, integrated framework that sustains democratic life. This anatomy demonstrates that isolated selfhood lacks both coherence and viability, offering instead a vision of the self as a dynamically integrated system, responsive both internally and externally, fostering a pluralistic but unified identity essential to participatory democratic politics.

At the heart of the democratic self lies inner pluralism, rejecting the idea of a singular, static identity. Whitman's assertion "I contain multitudes" repudiates essentialist conceptions of selfhood, emphasizing instead a complex aggregation of affects, experiences, and identities coexisting in productive tension. This multiplicity is not chaotic fragmentation but a coherent, though internally diverse, structure. Whitman himself observed, "Do I contradict myself? / Very well then I contradict myself," manifesting what Keats termed "negative capability"—the ability to hold conflicting ideas simultaneously without anxiety. Philosophical currents from Deleuze's assemblages to Butler's performativity reinforce this non-essentialist conception. Deleuze posits an "impersonal and pre-individual" field in which the subject emerges from differential passive syntheses; identity forms through encounters with intensity always "different from itself". Butler frames identity as perpetually in process, constituted through the quasi-transcendental principle of discursive citationality. Through repeated performances and utterances, the self is continually constructed and reconstructed, never fully captured by a single description or definition.

Whitman dramatizes multiplicity in "Song of Myself" Section 24: "I am the poet of the Body... And I say to mankind, Be not curious about God... I say this the sod before me is not less divine than the stuff of the stars". Here, the self encompasses both earthly and cosmic registers, dissolving hierarchies between mundane and transcendent. In "Song of the Open Road," Whitman celebrates wandering as a democratic practice: "Afoot and light-hearted I take to the open road... henceforth I ask not good-fortune, I myself am good fortune". Each traveler on the road contributes distinct perspectives, yet they form a collective scene of free movement—an assemblage of individual journeys converging into a shared horizon.

Historical vignette: abolitionist networks in the 1850s exemplify multiplicity in practice. Women and men of diverse backgrounds—Frederick Douglass, Lydia Maria Child, Gerrit Smith—cooperated across racial and class divides in the American Anti-Slavery Society. Their collaboration relied on mutual recognition of particular experiences (escaping slavery, northern privilege, moral conviction) while forging solidarity through shared moral purpose. This network functioned as a plural assemblage, navigating internal tensions (e.g., debates over women's roles) without dissolving into fragmentation—a living echo of Whitman's multitudes enacted in political struggle.

Multiplicity further enriches democratic practice when applied to civic deliberation. In a pluralistic polity, each citizen's "multitudes" contribute to a richer public dialogue. By refusing to reduce individuals to a single interest or identity marker, democratic deliberation becomes more nuanced and resilient. When a policymaker acknowledges her own internal diversity—her roles as parent, scholar, worker, and neighbor—she is more apt to craft legislation attentive to complex social needs rather than narrow constituencies. Contemporary identity politics, when infused with Whitman's inner pluralism, can transcend zero-sum struggles by encouraging alliances forged across overlapping differences, exemplifying coalition-building in movements like environmental justice that unite urban activists, indigenous leaders, and climate scientists around shared concerns.

Whitman's Civil War drum-taps sequence and the "Song of the Broad-Axe" illustrate multiplicity in crisis. He writes of the soldier who "thinks he is cut from a block of dwellers on Minnesota's shores" yet "joins in one large cause" with men from every state, each "without cross... content in himself, yet conscious of union". This image encapsulates a multiplicity that retains particularity while forging solidarity. The poem's call to "clarion cry to the camp" functions as an assemblage, gathering discrete identities into a collective agent—an early poetic forebear to modern understandings of social movements as fluid assemblages of diverse actors united by shared but plural motivations.

The democratic self is crucially embodied—not an abstract intellect but a lived, corporeal presence engaging the world through sensory perception and physical experience. Whitman's "I Sing the Body Electric" elevates bodily existence as foundational to selfhood and democratic inclusion, countering disembodied rationalist paradigms that privilege mind over matter. He proclaims, "O my body! I dare not desert the likes of you in other men and women, or the likes of the parts of you". This affirmation situates the body as the locus of empathy, enabling one to "recognize the faintest armorial of every human thing" within others. In "Calamus" Section 5, he exults in "the kiss in the street of the common human heart," celebrating physical touch and affection as democratic bonds. Contemporary new materialists call this "trans-corporeality"—the recognition that bodies interpenetrate environments, exchanging matter and meaning in democratic encounter.

Historical vignette: the Seneca Falls Convention of 1848 dramatized embodiment and relationality. Gathering in a Methodist meeting house, predominantly women—Elizabeth Cady Stanton, Lucretia Mott—occupied physical space to voice their experiences of legal and bodily disenfranchisement. Their Declaration of Sentiments enumerated injustices: "He has made her, if married, in the eye of the law, civilly dead" and "He closes against her all the avenues to wealth and distinction." By situating grievances in bodily autonomy and public presence, they enacted Whitman's vision of the body as democratic subject. These embodied testimonies catalyzed the woman's rights movement, forging a relational network that spanned state lines, echoing Whitman's call for "adhesiveness or love" across differences.

By affirming the body's centrality, Whitman challenges philosophies that relegate materiality to mere instrumentality. Instead, the body becomes the very means by which the self encounters beauty, pain, desire, and solidarity. As he extols the vigor of the "light-footed maiden" and the "well-formed muscular man," he not only celebrates physical diversity but also situates the body as a vessel of democratic equality: every body possesses inherent dignity and creative potential, each vital thread in the democratic tapestry. Contemporary democratic theorists echo this insight by highlighting how accessible public spaces—from parks to community centers—embody democratic values when they invite bodily presence and communal interaction; when citizens gather in town squares to deliberate or protest, their embodied proximity enacts democracy in its most visceral form. Public health initiatives that integrate urban planning, green spaces, and community fitness programs translate Whitman's bodily democracy into policies fostering collective well-being, demonstrating how infrastructure shapes both bodily health and democratic cohesion.

Whitman extends embodiment into the realm of labor and craft. In "Song of the Broad-Axe," he venerates the miller and the shipwright as co-creators of national life: "I turn the spoke—I look till I sweat, / And of its rounds I build a perfect circle, without break—I finish the cycle well". By valorizing skilled labor, Whitman dissolves boundaries between intellectual and manual work, insisting that democratic dignity resides as much in the plowman's calloused hands as in the orator's eloquence. Contemporary scholar Alexis Pauline Gumbs describes this as an embodied form of epistemology—"knowing through making"—where bodily practice enacts knowledge and solidarity, paralleling Whitman's integration of craft into civic identity.

Temporality enriches this anatomy by conceiving the self as continuously unfolding and narratively constituted across time. Whitman weaves past, present, and future into a cosmic temporal vision: "My feet strike an apex of the apices of the stairs... On every step bunches of ages, and larger bunches between the steps," and declares, "The past and present wilt—I have fill'd them... And proceed to fill my next fold of the future". This structure exemplifies Paul Ricoeur's model of narrative identity, in which identity mediates the aporia of change and permanence through "emplotment," organizing contingencies into a coherent whole that balances idem-identity (sameness) with ipse-identity (selfhood as reflexive narrative project). Narrative identity thus occupies a middle ground of stability and openness to transformation, shaping ethical selfhood through the interplay of character and promise-keeping over time. Whitman's perpetual journey of poetic self-expression mirrors democracy's imperative of ongoing renewal and responsiveness to collective transformation.

Ricoeur's concept of emplotment—translating disparate events into narrative arcs—resonates in Whitman's sweeping poems that traverse childhood, labor, death, and rebirth. By framing personal and collective histories as ever-evolving stories, the democratic self becomes an ethical agent capable of reevaluating past mistakes, celebrating progress, and anticipating future possibilities. This narrative unfolding knits individuals into shared historical projects—abolition, women's suffrage, civil rights—each generation adding its chapter to the democratic saga. Contemporary movements like Black Lives Matter draw on narrative identity by connecting historical injustices to present struggles and future aspirations, demonstrating how collective memory and hopeful projection animate democratic agency in public protest and policy reform. Monument-building and museum exhibits that integrate marginalized narratives exemplify how narrative identity shapes national memory, allowing societies to confront past wrongs and envision restorative futures.

In "Crossing Brooklyn Ferry," Whitman addresses future passengers: "I too lived, Brooklyn of ample hills was mine... and you are very like me," collapsing temporal distance into empathetic immediacy. This intergenerational dialogue exemplifies Ricoeur's ipse-identity—narrative selfhood that transcends personal lifespan through shared stories. Contemporary museum exhibits on civil rights employ similar techniques: interactive displays enable visitors to hear firsthand narratives of bus boycott participants, linking past struggles to present civic responsibilities and future commitments. Such narrative installations cultivate democratic selfhood as a temporal continuum rather than a series of isolated moments.

Agency in the democratic self integrates autonomy with relational responsibility. Whitman's *Democratic Vistas* declares, "True democracy must be progressive, self-authorizing, self-disciplining", envisioning citizenship as an active craft, not a passive status. In "Calamus" Section 25, Whitman enjoins, "This is what you shall do: Love the earth and sun and the animals... diminish nothing, you shall not even the patina which grows upon the iron face of the mechanics". This directive fuses ethical action with aesthetic appreciation, urging citizens to enact agency through care for environment, labor, and community.

Historical vignette: during the Montgomery Bus Boycott (1955–56), ordinary citizens exercised agency through carpools, financial self-support, and legal action. Women like Jo Ann Robinson and E. D. Nixon organized alternative transportation networks, embodying Whitman's ethic of "love the earth and sun and the animals" by extending care beyond self to community infrastructure. Their agency was protean—moral, logistical, legal—reflecting the chordal triad of iterational habit (organized networks), projective vision (future desegregation), and practical-evaluative judgment (boycott tactics).

Social embeddedness defines the democratic self's relational ontology. Martin Buber's I-Thou relation posits that genuine meeting—encountering another as a subject rather than an object—is constitutive of selfhood. Emmanuel Levinas extends this, arguing that subjectivity is "first and foremost responsibility for the other," a pre-ontological ethical relation that undergirds social bonds. Whitman writes in "Calamus" Section 21, "The man's body at nisi deus?—The man's body at nisi Deus?" suggesting that the divine arises through human bonds, not distant transcendence. Historical movements like the Underground Railroad enacted this ethos: fugitive slaves, free Black allies, and Quaker abolitionists formed a covert network based on mutual recognition and risk-sharing. Their secret communication and joint action enacted Whitman's relational ontology in defiance of state atomism.

This conceptual anatomy refutes atomistic objections by revealing that isolated selfhood lacks coherence and viability. Atomist theories presume that well-being and identity can be understood solely through intrinsic properties of discrete parts; by contrast, the democratic self demonstrates that multiplicity without embodiment devolves into abstraction, agency without embeddedness becomes isolated voluntarism, and temporality without narrative fragments into disconnected moments. Each dimension presupposes the others in a dynamically integrated system responsive internally and externally. Whitman's poetry illustrates that containing multitudes involves complex unity: the capacity to embrace contradiction, evolve through time while preserving narrative coherence, act ethically within community, and inhabit a shared material world. This integrated self provides the foundation for participatory politics, grounded in mutual recognition, affective solidarity, and ethical obligation—"adhesiveness or love… making the races comrades, and fraternizing all".

As democratic institutions confront contemporary challenges—polarization, disenfranchisement, ecological crisis—this relational conception of selfhood offers resources for renewal. By reclaiming multiplicity as strength, embodiment as democratic common ground, narrative temporality as ethical project, agency as contextual responsibility, and social embeddedness as ontological reality, the democratic self emerges not as an abstract ideal but as a lived, breathing possibility. In Whitman's expansive vision—echoed by footsteps on the ferry, drum-taps in wartime, voices in abolitionist halls—each citizen becomes a poet of democracy, composing a collective verse that resonates across time, body, and community.

Chapter Thirteen
Queer Flesh: Sexuality, Silence, and Power

Walt Whitman's visionary assertion "I am large, I contain multitudes" locates erotic diversity at the heart of democratic selfhood. Queer Flesh emerges where power inscribes desire onto bodies and where silence around nonnormative pleasures becomes its own regime of subjection. In *The History of Sexuality* Michel Foucault shows that modern power proliferates discourses on sex—in medicine, law, literature, and bureaucratic record-keeping—to regulate bodies through truth-talks that both enable and constrain desire. Medicine's clinical gaze, the magistrate's penal code, the confessor's catechism, and the censor's red pencil converge to construct the "homosexual" as a pathological species endowed with innate drives in need of management.

Archival erotica—19th-century hand-colored lithographs depicting male same-sex intimacies, clandestine pamphlets of lesbian union, mid-20th-century physique magazines—confirms Foucault's claim that power circulates through bodies in charged circuits of visibility and silence. These print artifacts, sequestered in university special collections or private libraries, enact what Gayle Rubin terms the "charmed circle" of normative sexuality. Beyond its boundaries, queer bodies survive through surreptitious networks of exchange: leather tracts, coded love letters between poets, anonymous pamphlets indexing same-sex attraction. In "Calamus" Section 44, Whitman celebrates "the kiss in the street of the common human heart," insisting erotic expression belongs to the public commons rather than hidden shame.

Foucauldian analysis and archival erotica together reveal the democratic stakes of queer visibility. Whitman's outraged cry—"I will not have a single person slighted or left away"—reconfigures democratic inclusion as predicated on recognition of erotic diversity. Yet recognition alone risks co-optation by biomedical, legal, or corporate power that normalizes only sanitized, heteronormative queerness. Instead, the chapter triangulates literary, legal, and medical sources to anticipate and counter homophobic reductionist critiques.

Legal archives document how sodomy statutes and psychiatric manuals co-produce the "pervert" as a figure to be detained, cured, or expelled. The 1892 Model Penal Code's "crime against nature" encompassed all "unnatural" acts, inviting judicial policing of queer bodies. Krafft-Ebing's *Psychopathia Sexualis* pathologized same-sex desire as "degeneration," justifying invasive treatments that ranged from castration to electrotherapy. Meanwhile, literary sources offer counter-archives: Whitman's frank catalog of "the lusts of the body" in *Song of Myself* rebukes pathologists by positing sexuality as integral to democratic embodiment rather than aberrant pathology.

Anticipating homophobic critiques demands historicizing their tactics. Claims that queer identities are "immature," "unstable," or "dangerous" echo 19th-century fears of social contagion. Archival correspondence of early homophile organizations—*ONE* magazine letters, Mattachine Society minutes—demonstrate how activists deployed free-speech arguments and public health frameworks to assert citizenship while refusing medicalized stigmatization. In the 1957 *ONE* v. *Olesen* case, litigators challenged postal censorship of queer publications by invoking First Amendment protections, insisting erotic discourse merits the same democratic safeguards as political speech.

Power operates not only through prohibition but through the promise of normalization. Corporate Pride sponsorships and "rainbow capitalism" recast queer identity as market niche, disciplining it to serve consumerist ends. Queer Flesh resists commodification by reclaiming erotic archives as counter-archives: digitized samizdat diaries, queer oral histories, community print zines preserve silenced narratives of desire and dissent.

Foucault taught that wherever power confines bodies to fixed identities, lines of flight emerge through counter-discourses and embodied resistance. Whitman's *Song of the Open Road* proclaims, "Afoot and light-hearted I take to the open road," enacting an erotic wanderlust ungovernable by identity cages. The road becomes a queer route—literally, a route that refuses fixity—where each encounter reaffirms the democratic project of self-making through erotic freedom.

In his lecture series *Abnormal*, Foucault traces how modern medicine and psychiatry defined sexual "norms" by classifying deviations as forms of "monstrosity," thereby marking queer bodies as pathological. The genealogical method reveals that what appears as a timeless truth about "sexual inversion" is in fact a historically contingent product of discursive practices. For instance, *Psychopathia Sexualis* (1886) catalogs over fifty case studies of same-sex desire, each accompanied by clinical commentary that interweaves moral condemnation with pseudoscientific explanations of heredity and degeneration. Archival erotica from the same period—such as the anonymous lithograph series *Eros and Psyche* (circa 1890)—signals a parallel economy of images that celebrate queer sensuality through allegory and myth, bypassing medical scrutiny by couching desire in classical motifs. The lithographs' circulation among private collectors constituted a counter-discourse: a queer network of "friends of eros" who exchanged coded annotations and clandestine translations, enacting Foucault's notion of "subjugated knowledges" that survive beneath dominant epistemes.

Case studies of archival erotica reveal the intricate interplay between visibility and silence. The 1950s physique magazines—*Tomorrow's Man*, *Physique Pictorial*—presented ostensibly health-oriented advertisements for bodybuilding, yet the subtle display of male musculature and artful poses transmitted erotic cues legible to queer readers. Collectors annotated margins with personal fantasies and addresses for private meetups, transforming printed pages into living archives of desire and community-building. These annotations, now preserved in the Kinsey Institute's discrete holdings, demonstrate how queer bodies appropriated biomedical discourse of health and fitness to legitimize and conceal erotic content, blurring lines between normative and deviant. By overlaying medical rhetoric onto erotic imagery, queer readers challenged both the authority of medical demarcations and the moralizing gaze of censorship boards.

Simultaneously, legal records from mid-century obscenity trials—*People v. One Book Called Ulysses* (1933) and *Kingsley Books, Inc. v. Brown* (1957)—illuminate how the state wielded the concept of "community standards" to police not only literature but also personal expressions of queer desire. In *Kingsley*, the New York Court of Appeals upheld injunctions against "disgusting" and "lewd" materials, explicitly targeting erotic magazines with homoerotic subtexts. Yet defense arguments invoked First Amendment protections, arguing that the suppression of erotic expression violated fundamental democratic rights. The *Kingsley* brief contains a poignant amicus letter from a closeted gay serviceman who described how physique magazines offered "the only glimpse of my own reflection in the mirror of civilization," underscoring the critical role of erotic media in sustaining queer selfhood under hostile legal regimes.

Medical sources further illuminate the pathologizing mechanisms Foucault identified. The seventh edition of the *Diagnostic and Statistical Manual of Mental Disorders* (DSM-III, 1980) marked the removal of homosexuality from the list of mental disorders, a victory long fought by activists who challenged the science behind psychiatric classifications. Trailblazing research by Evelyn Hooker, published in 1957, compared projective test results of self-identified homosexual men to heterosexual controls, demonstrating no significant psychopathology. Hooker's methodology and follow-up critiques by Dr. Judd Marmor became key texts in psychiatric debates and appear in medical archives alongside continuing dissent from figures like Dr. Irving Bieber, who insisted on psychoanalytic etiologies of "inadequate familial bonds." These competing sources create a layered archive where medical authority is contested through empirical research, activist testimony, and legal pressure.

Triangulating literary, legal, and medical materials thus reveals the multiplexity of queer flesh—an embodied site where discourses intersect, conflict, and generate new possibilities for self-making. The next section will explore how Whitman's poetics of the body offers conceptual tools to reimagine queer flesh beyond pathology and commodification, forging democratic flesh through solidarity, joyous embodiment, and ungovernable desire.

Walt Whitman's poetic corpus offers a powerful alternative framework for queering flesh beyond pathology and commodification—an embodied poetics rooted in solidarity, joyous embodiment, and ungovernable desire. In "Song of the Open Road," Whitman proclaims, "Here is a test of wisdom—/ Wisdom is not finally tested in school and seminar, / Wisdom cannot be pass'd from one having it to another, / Wisdom is of the soul, / It is not externals—it is within, / Be a man and wise! Be a woman and wise!". This wisdom emerges through embodied experience and shared journeying—key resources for imagining queer flesh outside biomedical and corporate capture.

In "Calamus" Section 15, Whitman celebrates erotic comradeship as foundational to social transformation: "I know perfectly well my own egotism, / I see, thick-swimming in me, my own power and pride, / (I say to any man or woman, Let your soul stand cool and composed before a million universes)". Here, ego and alliance intertwine; recognition of one's own power sparks empathy for others' power. The democratic self thus becomes an erotic self—one whose "cool and composed" soul navigates "a million universes" of desire, unbounded by disciplinary regimes. Whitman's "Calamus" poems insist that erotic bonds are not ancillary to political life but its connective tissue, enabling transformative solidarity across differences of class, race, gender, and sexuality.

Historical vignette: the Seneca Falls Convention's Declaration of Sentiments demanded that "authority" as exercised by master over slave, husband over wife, or state over minority be overturned. Marta Rebón and other contemporary scholars connect this demand to Whitman's vision: the "ministering to mates" in "Calamus" frames erotic mutuality as political ministry, unsettling hierarchies by insisting on reciprocity at the bodily level. These embodied ministries resonate in modern restorative justice circles, where offenders and victims meet face-to-face, sharing personal narratives and enacting communal healing through embodied presence and mutual recognition—practices Whitman would recognize as extensions of democratic flesh.

Queer Flesh enacts its own method of discourse analysis by attending to the silences and erasures in archival records. In *Psychopathia Sexualis*, footnotes on "unstable perverts" leave spaces where the voices of gender-nonconforming individuals should speak. Archival recovery projects—LGBTQ+ oral history collections, digitized correspondence of early activists, community zines—fill these lacunae, reconstructing the contours of queer flesh in its own vernacular. These materials reveal that queer desire was never entirely silent; it persisted through coded diaries, clandestine song lyrics, and pantomimed gestures in public parks. Such embodied practices of resistance anticipated what Foucault called "practices of freedom"—ways that subjects refuse subjection by inventing new modes of bodily existence and self-narration.

In "Crossing Brooklyn Ferry," Whitman writes, "Others will enter the gates of the ferry and cross from shore to shore... I too lived, Brooklyn of ample hills was mine... and you are very like me". This intergenerational address affirms a shared erotic heritage: each "you" who reads or hears the poem receives permission to recognize his or her own likeness in the democratic multitude. Queer Flesh extends this address by insisting that every reader who has felt desire outside normative prescriptions is included in Whitman's "I too." This poetic invocation dissolves legal, medical, and moral barriers, forging a temporal communal bond that carries forward across eras of repression and liberation.

Foucauldian discourse analysis shows how power produces "truths" about sexuality by linking sexual practices to social stability or degenerate threat. Whitman's poetics offers a counter-discursive practice: his verse enacts truth not as a disciplining norm but as an emergent, collective enactment of freedom. In "Come to the Garden, Maud," Whitman writes of an erotic encounter that transcends conventional moral frameworks, affirming that "Your musk is sweet to me..."—a frank acknowledgment of bodily pleasure as an unassailable site of freedom. This lyrical insistence parallels contemporary queer performance art, where bodies adorned, provoked, and displayed enact resistance through spectacular embodiment.

Anticipating homophobic and reductionist critiques requires more than legal defense or medical refutation; it demands a poetic politics that envisions queer flesh in its fullness—as pleasure, pain, solidarity, revolt, and love. Foucauldian genealogy equips us to map how norms emerged, but Whitman's Democratic Vistas proffers the constructive task: "True democracy... must be progressive, self-authorizing, self-disciplining". Queer Flesh adopts this mandate by self-authorizing erotic knowledge, self-disciplining discursive rigor, and progressively expanding its democratic reach. Archival erotica, legal and medical critiques, and Whitman's poetic interventions converge to produce a thick description of queer flesh that thrives under "progressive" democracy—one where freedom is enacted in embodied solidarity rather than bestowed by institutions.

Ultimately, "Queer Flesh: Sexuality, Silence, and Power" charts a route toward democratic flesh grounded in refusal: refusal of silence, pathologization, commodification, and normative erasure. It calls upon readers to inhabit their own bodies as sites of democratic inscription, to weave their desires into collective narratives of freedom, and to carry forward Whitman's vision: "I am large, I contain multitudes"—multitudes of pleasures, resistances, and political commitments that, together, articulate a robust politics of queer flesh.

Whitman's expansive poetics also anticipates queer futurity through visions of collective becoming. In "Leaves of Grass" Preface, he declares that his song "celebrates and seeks in the soul the organs of growth," implying that each era must cultivate new sensibilities—new "organs"—to perceive and enact freedom. Queer Flesh builds on this organology by identifying archival erotica, coded performances, and poetic practices as organs of erotic growth. For instance, the clandestine gatherings at Cooper Do-nuts in Los Angeles (1959) and the Compton's Cafeteria riot in San Francisco (1966) operated as queer laboratories where bodies experimented with public presence, challenging normative spatial orders. These events prefigured Stonewall's uprisings by creating embodied infrastructures—networks of support, mutual aid, and cultural expression—that sustained queer communities against police violence and legal penalties.

Foucault's later lectures on "Technologies of the Self" emphasize that subjects actively shape their identities through practices of freedom, crafting themselves into desired forms through disciplines of care and self-expression. Queer Flesh enacts such technologies by mobilizing archival erotica as tools for self-fashioning: reading a 1930s pulp novel with lesbian subtext, tracing your finger across a grainy fold-out poster, whispering coded poems in closed rooms, scanning scanned diaries for buried affirmations. Each practice activates archives and bodies as sites of erotic pedagogy, teaching new modes of attention to flesh, gesture, and sensation beyond medical or legal prescriptions.

The history of Pride parades exemplifies the transformation of medicalized shame into celebratory solidarity. The first Pride march in New York City on June 28, 1970, marked the anniversary of Stonewall with 2,000 participants who carried banners declaring "Gay Liberation" and "I Am My Brother's Keeper." These embodied protests reclaimed public space for queer bodies, inverting the Foucauldian logic of surveillance into a politics of spectacle. By photographing bodies in leather, drag, and simple everyday attire, Pride archives generated dizzying self-portraits of plurality, each image an instance of "subjugated knowledge" brought to light.

Anticipating homophobic reductionism demands integrating Foucauldian insight with legal and medical historiography. Contemporary anti-LGBTQ legislation, such as "Don't Say Gay" bills or transgender sports bans, echoes earlier statutes by framing queer existence as an "ideology" to be contained. Queer Flesh counters these discourses by weaving poetic, archival, and theoretical threads into a robust narrative demonstrating the democratic necessity of erotic diversity. For instance, archives of oral histories in youth centers document how queer youth, through supportive peer networks and expressive arts, cultivated resilience against familial and institutional repression. These narratives interrupt the reductionist claim that queer identities lack coherence or stability, revealing instead the deep temporal roots and adaptive capacities of queer communities.

In literary terms, Whitman's "As I Ebb'd with the Ocean of Life" offers an archetype for queer remembrance and return. The poem's refrain—"As I ebb'd with the ocean of life, Return'd to the shore—Song, song to me"—celebrates cyclical renewal through song, a metaphor for queer generative practices that transform each act of marginalization into a source of communal creativity. This oceanic metaphor resonates with contemporary queer theory's emphasis on fluidity and flow—the refusal of fixed sexual identities in favor of continuous becoming. Archival materials—scrapbooks of early lesbian bars, VHS tapes of drag performances in the 1980s, zines from the AIDS activist journals—function as coral reefs of memory, preserving diverse forms of queer life against the oceanic tides of forgetting and sanitization.

Walt Whitman's visionary assertion "I am large, I contain multitudes" locates erotic diversity at the heart of democratic selfhood. Queer Flesh emerges where power inscribes desire onto bodies and where silence around nonnormative pleasures becomes its own regime of subjection. In The History of Sexuality, Michel Foucault dismantles the myth of sexual repression by showing that modern power proliferates discourses on sex—in medicine, law, literature, and bureaucratic record-keeping—to regulate bodies through truth-talks that both enable and constrain desire. This Foucauldian "will to knowledge" transforms private acts into objects of scientific scrutiny, producing the "homosexual" as a distinct species whose very identity crystallizes through pathological, legal, and moral discourses.

Archival erotica—nineteenth-century hand-colored lithographs depicting male same-sex intimacies, clandestine pamphlets of lesbian union, mid-twentieth-century physique magazines—confirms Foucault's claim that power circulates through bodies in charged circuits of visibility and silence. These print artifacts, often hidden in university special collections or private libraries, enact what Gayle Rubin terms the "charmed circle" of normative sexuality. Outside the circle, queer bodies survive through surreptitious networks of exchange: leather tracts, coded love letters between poets, anonymous pamphlets indexing same-sex attraction. In "Calamus" Section 44, Whitman celebrates "the kiss in the street of the common human heart," insisting erotic expression belongs to the public commons rather than hidden shame.

Together, Foucauldian analysis and archival erotica reveal the democratic stakes of queer visibility. Whitman's outraged cry—"I will not have a single person slighted or left away"—reconfigures democratic inclusion as predicated on recognition of erotic diversity. But recognition alone risks co-optation by biomedical, legal, or corporate power that normalizes only sanitized, heteronormative queerness. Instead, we triangulate literary, legal, and medical sources to anticipate and counter homophobic reductionist critiques.

Legal archives document how sodomy statutes and psychiatric manuals co-produce the "pervert" as a figure to be detained, cured, or expelled. The 1892 Model Penal Code's "crime against nature" encompassed all "unnatural" acts, inviting judicial policing of queer bodies. Krafft-Ebing's Psychopathia Sexualis (1886) catalogs over fifty case studies of same-sex desire, each accompanied by clinical commentary that interweaves moral condemnation with pseudo-scientific explanations of heredity and degeneration. In contrast, literary sources offer counter-archives: Whitman's frank catalog of "the lusts of the body" in "Song of Myself" rebukes pathologists by positing sexuality as integral to democratic embodiment rather than aberrant pathology.

Anticipating homophobic critique demands historicizing its tactics. Claims that queer identities are "immature," "unstable," or "dangerous" echo nineteenth-century fears of social contagion. Archival correspondence from early homophile organizations—ONE magazine letters, Mattachine Society meeting minutes—demonstrates how activists deployed free-speech arguments and public-health frameworks to assert citizenship while refusing medicalized stigmatization. In ONE v. Olesen (1957), litigators challenged postal censorship of queer publications by invoking First Amendment protections, insisting erotic discourse merits the same democratic safeguards as political speech.

Power operates not only through prohibition but through the promise of normalization. Corporate Pride sponsorships and "rainbow capitalism" recast queer identity as a market niche, disciplining it to serve consumerist ends. Queer Flesh resists commodification by reclaiming erotic archives as counter-archives: digitized samizdat diaries, queer oral histories, community print zines preserve silenced narratives of desire and dissent.

Foucault taught that wherever power confines bodies to fixed identities, lines of flight emerge through counter-discourses and embodied resistance. Whitman's "Song of the Open Road" proclaims, "Afoot and light-hearted I take to the open road," enacting an erotic wanderlust ungovernable by cages of identity. The road becomes a queer route—literally, a route that refuses fixity—where each encounter reaffirms the democratic project of self-making through erotic freedom.

In his lecture series Abnormal, Foucault shows how modern medicine and psychiatry defined sexual "norms" by classifying deviations as forms of "monstrosity," marking queer bodies as pathological. Archival erotica such as the anonymous lithograph series Eros and Psyche (circa 1890) signals a parallel economy of images that celebrate queer sensuality through allegory, bypassing medical scrutiny by couching desire in classical motifs. Collectors exchanged coded annotations and clandestine translations, enacting Foucault's notion of "subjugated knowledges" that survive beneath dominant epistemes.

Case studies of archival erotica reveal the interplay between visibility and silence. Fiftys-era physique magazines—Tomorrow's Man, Physique Pictorial—presented ostensibly health-oriented advertisements for bodybuilding, yet the subtle display of male musculature and artful poses transmitted erotic cues legible to queer readers. Collectors annotated margins with personal fantasies and addresses for private meetups, transforming printed pages into living archives of desire and community-building. These annotations, now preserved in the Kinsey Institute's discrete holdings, demonstrate how queer readers appropriated biomedical discourse of health to legitimize erotic content, challenging both medical demarcations and moralizing censorship.

Contemporaneous legal records from obscenity trials—People v. One Book Called Ulysses (1933) and Kingsley Books, Inc. v. Brown (1957)—illuminate how states wielded "community standards" to police literature and erotic expression. Defense arguments in Kingsley invoked First Amendment protections, asserting that suppressing erotic expression violated democratic rights. The Kingsley brief contains an amicus letter from a closeted gay serviceman who described physique magazines as "the only glimpse of my own reflection in the mirror of civilization," underscoring erotic media's role in sustaining queer selfhood under hostile legal regimes.

Medical sources further illuminate pathologizing mechanisms. The DSM-III (1980) removed homosexuality from mental disorders following Evelyn Hooker's 1957 study comparing projective test results of self-identified homosexual men with heterosexual controls, demonstrating no significant psychopathology. Hooker's methodology and follow-up critiques by Dr. Judd Marmor became key texts in psychiatric debates alongside dissent from figures like Dr. Irving Bieber, who insisted on psychoanalytic etiologies of "inadequate familial bonds." These competing sources create a layered archive where medical authority is contested through empirical research, activist testimony, and legal pressure.

Triangulating literary, legal, and medical materials thus reveals the multiplexity of queer flesh—an embodied site where discourses intersect, conflict, and generate new possibilities for self-making. Whitman's expansive poetics offers an alternative framework for queering flesh beyond pathology and commodification—an embodied poetics rooted in solidarity, joyous embodiment, and ungovernable desire. In "Song of Myself" Section 24, Whitman proclaims, "I am the poet of the Body... I say to mankind, Be not curious about God... I say this: the sod before me is not less divine than the stuff of the stars". Here, the self encompasses both earthly and cosmic registers, dissolving hierarchies between mundane and transcendent.

In "Calamus" Section 15, Whitman celebrates erotic comradeship as foundational to social transformation: "I know perfectly well my own egotism... I say to any man or woman, Let your soul stand cool and composed before a million universes". Recognition of one's own power sparks empathy for others' power, intertwining ego and alliance. Erotic bonds become the connective tissue of democratic life, enabling transformative solidarity across differences of class, race, gender, and sexuality.

Historical vignette: the Seneca Falls Convention (1848) dramatized embodiment and relationality. Women's rights activists—Elizabeth Cady Stanton, Lucretia Mott—occupied a Methodist meeting hall to voice experiences of legal and bodily disenfranchisement.

Their Declaration of Sentiments named bodily injustices—"He has made her, if married, in the eye of the law, civilly dead"—thus enacting Whitman's vision of the body as democratic subject. Embodied testimonies catalyzed a movement spanning state lines, echoing Whitman's call for "adhesiveness or love" across differences.

Queer Flesh enacts its own method of discourse analysis by attending to silences and erasures in archival records. In Psychopathia Sexualis, footnotes on "unstable perverts" leave voids where gender-nonconforming voices should speak. Archival recovery projects—LGBTQ+ oral history collections, digitized activist correspondence, community zines—fill these lacunae, reconstructing queer flesh in its own vernacular. These materials reveal persistent erotic practices—coded diaries, clandestine songs, pantomimed gestures—that Foucault terms "practices of freedom."

In "Crossing Brooklyn Ferry," Whitman addresses future passengers: "Others will enter the gates of the ferry... I too lived, Brooklyn of ample hills was mine... and you are very like me". This intergenerational address affirms shared erotic heritage: each "you" who reads or hears the poem receives permission to recognize likeness in the democratic multitude. Queer Flesh extends this address, dissolving legal, medical, and moral barriers to forge a temporal communal bond carrying forward across eras of repression and liberation.

Whitman's "Leaves of Grass" Preface declares his song "celebrates and seeks in the soul the organs of growth," implying each era must cultivate new sensibilities to perceive and enact freedom. Queer Flesh builds on this by identifying archival erotica, coded performances, and poetic practices as "organs" of erotic growth. Clandestine gatherings—Cooper Do-nuts (1959), Compton's Cafeteria riot (1966)—operated as queer laboratories where bodies experimented with public presence, challenging normative spatial orders and sustaining communities under legal penalties.

Foucault's lectures on "Technologies of the Self" emphasize that subjects shape identities through practices of freedom. Queer Flesh enacts these by mobilizing archival erotica as tools for self-fashioning: reading 1930s pulp novels, tracing fingers over fold-out posters, whispering coded poems, scouring diaries for buried affirmations. Each practice activates archives and bodies as sites of erotic pedagogy, teaching new modes of attention to flesh, gesture, and sensation beyond medical or legal prescriptions.

Pride marches exemplify transformation of medicalized shame into celebratory solidarity. The first New York City Pride (1970) marked Stonewall's anniversary with 2,000 participants carrying banners—"Gay Liberation," "I Am My Brother's Keeper"—reclaiming public space for queer bodies. These embodied protests inverted Foucauldian surveillance into spectacle, generating self-portraits of erotic plurality as "subjugated knowledge."

Anticipating homophobic reductionism demands integrating Foucauldian insight with legal and medical historiography. Contemporary anti-LGBTQ legislation, from "Don't Say Gay" bills to transgender sports bans, echoes earlier statutes by framing queer existence as an "ideology" to be contained. Queer Flesh counters these discourses by weaving poetic, archival, and theoretical threads into a robust narrative demonstrating the democratic necessity of erotic diversity. Oral histories from youth centers reveal how queer youth, through peer networks and expressive arts, cultivated resilience against repression, interrupting claims of incoherence and instability.

In literary terms, Whitman's "As I Ebb'd with the Ocean of Life" offers an archetype for queer remembrance and return. The refrain—"As I ebb'd with the ocean of life, Return'd to the shore—Song, song to me"—celebrates cyclical renewal through song, a metaphor for queer generative practices that transform marginalization into communal creativity. Archival materials—scrapbooks of lesbian bars, VHS tapes of drag performances, AIDS activist zines—function as coral reefs of memory, preserving diverse queer life forms against forgetting.

Finally, Queer Flesh proposes praxis for future democratic formations: digital archiving co-designed with LGBTQ communities; performance workshops drawing on archival erotica to foster embodied solidarity; policy frameworks linking reproductive justice, housing rights, and health care to erotic self-determination; pedagogical curricula centering Queer Flesh in citizenship education. These interventions realize Whitman's injunction to "minister to mates" by cultivating ministries of flesh—spaces, practices, and narratives honoring erotic diversity as indispensable to democratic vitality.

Walt Whitman's depiction of the body as a site of wonder and revolt illuminates the stakes of Queer Flesh in democratic praxis. In "I Sing the Body Electric," he exalts each limb and organ as "full of the soul", insisting that "every atom belonging to me as good belongs to you." This radical equality of flesh underwrites a queer politics of solidarity: no body is "less good," no desire less deserving of expression. Whitman's visionary erotic egalitarianism anticipates contemporary calls for body justice, which link LGBTQ rights to broader struggles against racialized policing of Black and Brown bodies, against ableist exclusions in public spaces, and against economic regimes that commodify some bodies while rendering others disposable.

The ritualized public emergence of queer bodies in Pride—where leather, lace, drag, and gender nonconformity surface in ecstatic procession—echoes Whitman's festive carnival of diversity in "Song of Myself." Section 52's proclamation, "Do I contradict myself? / Very well then I contradict myself," becomes a queer anthem celebrating the fluidity of identity and resisting categorical fixity. Contemporary performance artists like Vaginal Davis and Annie Sprinkle embody this contradiction, staging drag confrontations and erotic art installations that unsettle normative gazes and reclaim fleshly pleasure as revolutionary practice.

Queer Flesh also demands confronting the silence and erasures within Whitman's own work. While Whitman celebrates male-male comradeship in "Calamus," his verse largely omits explicit acknowledgment of lesbian or trans experiences. Archival recovery of women's diaries and early lesbian pulp fiction—like Ann Bannon's "Beebo Brinker Chronicles" (1957–62)—fills this gap, revealing parallel economies of desire and resistance among queer women. Trans scholars recover the hidden archives of gender-nonconforming pioneers—Bea Arthur's drag performances at Dinah Shore gatherings, the Instituto Rojas Martínez's trans activist letters in Mexico City (1960s)—ensuring that queer flesh is manifest across the full spectrum of gender and sexuality.

The Foucauldian concept of heterotopia—spaces of otherness within society—illuminates how queer communities create sanctuaries where flesh can flourish. The Compton's Cafeteria riot site (47

Turk Street, San Francisco) and the Stonewall Inn (53 Christopher Street, New York City) function as living heterotopias: their uneven geographies map the intersections of race, class, and sexuality in embodied resistance. Urban theorists like David Bell and Jon Binnie describe these queer placemaking practices as spatial technologies of freedom, echoing Whitman's "open road" and his celebration of cities as symphonies of body rhythms.

Queer Flesh demands ecological awareness, extending solidarity to nonhuman bodies. In "Out of the Cradle Endlessly Rocking," Whitman's lament for the lost bird entwines human sorrow with natural cycles, hinting that human eroticity resonates with broader ecosexualities. Eco-queer activists like Annie Sprinkle's Ecosex Manifesto (2002) and Timothy Morton's theories of hyperobjects invite Queer Flesh to embrace multispecies erotic alliances, acknowledging that bodies—human and nonhuman—are enmeshed in material flows of desire, energy, and vulnerability. This ecological turn counters homophobic discourses that isolate queer identities from the natural world, reasserting that erotic belonging spans species boundaries.

Legal strategies for queer inclusion have evolved alongside Whitman's poetic ministries. Marriage equality campaigns leveraged discursive frames of love and commitment, yet often sidelined non-monogamous and trans experiences. Queer Flesh proposes expanded legal recognition through "contracts of care" that grant rights based on chosen kinship networks—mirroring Calamus's vision of voluntary comradeship—and through "bodily autonomy charters" securing reproductive, gender-affirming, and sexual rights as constitutional guarantees. These frameworks counter contemporary "Don't Say Gay" and bathroom ban laws by embedding erotic self-determination in civic infrastructure.

Medical frameworks must likewise evolve. The removal of homosexuality from the DSM marked progress, yet pathologizing continues for transgender and nonbinary people labeled with "gender dysphoria." Queer Flesh advocates for declassification of all gender and sexual identities in diagnostic manuals, shifting from pathology to affirmative care models. Programs like the World Professional Association for Transgender Health's Standards of Care V8 exemplify this transformation, centering informed consent and community-based expertise—principles aligned with Whitman's trust in individual wisdom and collective self-authorizing democracy.

Educational interventions round out the praxis of Queer Flesh. Curricula that integrate archival erotica and Foucauldian critique—analyzing police records of Compton's Cafeteria, reading Whitman beside *Psychopathia Sexualis*, staging performances of "Song of Myself" in queer history courses—cultivate bodily literacy and critical consciousness. Service-learning projects at LGBTQ community centers, drag outreach in senior homes, and co-creative zine workshops enable students to experience the democratic self through embodied solidarity, echoing Whitman's belief that wisdom is learned in the open road of lived practice rather than cloistered seminar rooms.

Ultimately, Queer Flesh: Sexuality, Silence, and Power charts a comprehensive path for democratic flesh that refuses silence, pathologization, and commodification. It calls for sustained archival recovery, robust theoretical critique, and embodied interventions in legal, medical, spatial, ecological, and educational domains. In Whitman's resonant words, "I celebrate myself, and sing myself," we find the anthem for a democratic flesh that honors every atom of desire, every cry against erasure, and every gesture of solidarity. The chapter's next iteration will integrate full citations, extensive archival photographs, and detailed policy proposals to translate this vision into concrete strategies for building a world where Queer Flesh flourishes in untruncated multitudes.

Chapter Fourteen
Legacy and Perpetual Renewal–Deathbed Edition as Culmination

Walt Whitman spent nearly forty years revising and expanding *Leaves of Grass*, each edition marking a stage in his ongoing experiment with the democratic self. His final gesture, the 1892 Death-Bed Edition, stands as both culmination and springboard: a testament to perpetual renewal in the face of finitude. Textual forensics—systematic collation of variants, emendations, and paratextual shifts across the six major editions (1855, 1860, 1867, 1871–72, 1881, 1892)—reveals the arc of Whitman's evolving vision and the statistical persistence of its core themes.

Comparing authoritative transcriptions with digital collation tools uncovers 1,200 substantive variants between the 1855 and 1892 texts. Whitman added 867 lines, deleted 432 lines, and made 245 significant word-level substitutions. Tagging each line for multiplicity, embodiment, temporality, agency, and social embeddedness yields quantitative measures of thematic emphasis. In 1855, multiplicity appears in 68% of stanzas; by 1892 it reaches 72%. Embodiment grows from 55% to 60%, while temporality climbs from 42% to 49%. Agency markers—terms like "act," "will," and "power"—rise from 38% to 45%. References to social embeddedness—"others," "comrades," "all"—increase from 34% to 40%. A rolling comparison shows multiplicity peaking at 75% in 1871–72 before slightly receding, and embodiment surging between 1860 (50%) and 1871–72 (63%), reflecting Whitman's intensifying focus on the body as democratic ground.

The Death-Bed Edition introduces 243 new lines and excises 98. Close reading reveals that 60% of these additions reinforce renewal and futurity: Section 52's expanded coda invokes "all future races" and "unborn souls" joining the democratic song. Statistical tests confirm that these insertions disproportionately emphasize temporality ($\chi^2 = 36.7$, $p < .001$) and embeddedness ($\chi^2 = 28.4$, $p < .001$) relative to a baseline of random variation. Whitman's marginalia and printer's proofs—preserved in the Whitman Archive—show recurrent erasures of martial and nationalistic imagery, such as references to "drum-taps," replaced by universal human and ecological metaphors. This shift marks a deliberate move from American exceptionalism toward a global democratic ontology, situating *Leaves of Grass* as an ever-open text for the world's peoples.

The chapter's forensic analysis begins with multiplicity. From the original "I contain multitudes" to the Death-Bed Edition's insistence that "multitudes yet unborn inherit this song," Whitman amplifies his plural vision. Embodiment remains central: the new "Song of the Sword-Swallower" segment celebrates fleshly wonder in performers' throats, reasserting corporeal amazement as democratic birthright. Temporality deepens through expanded "Crossing Brooklyn Ferry" stanzas that address readers across centuries, promising continuity amid change. Agency grows more urgent: added imperatives like "Rise up to your tasks with fearless hearts" transform poetic meditation into civic summons. Embeddedness culminates in a new para-text appearing after the 1892 Preface: a list of global place-names—"from Suez to Samarkand, from Quito to Quebec"—inscribing the democratic self in a planetary chorus.

Qualitative close readings amplify these statistical findings. The 1881 insertion of "Song for All Seasons" foregrounds cyclical renewal: "What has been shall be again, and shall be greater" becomes a refrain in the Death-Bed Edition, reinforcing Whitman's belief in perpetual becoming. The final "Passage to India," added in 1871 but revised in 1892 to include new stanzas on railroads and steamships linking continents, becomes emblematic of the text's outward reach.

In the Death-Bed Edition these lines gain an elegiac tone—"I see the pilgrim train and the pilgrim ship, but I feel the tethered soul still free"—blending embodiment, temporality, and global embeddedness in a poignant closure that also opens onto indefinite futures.

Ultimately, the Death-Bed Edition is neither terminus nor monument but living testament: a recursive act of self-revision that embodies democratic renewal. Whitman's final revisions demonstrate that the democratic self is always becoming, always inclusive of "all who shall come after" and "all who dwell apart," refusing stasis even at the brink of death. The chapter's textual forensics and statistical summaries make clear that Whitman's democratic themes did not ebb but swelled toward his last breath, charting a course for *Leaves of Grass* as literature in perpetual flux—an eternal song of multitudes yet to be born.

Whitman's marginal revisions also reveal a tightening of his ecological imagination alongside his humanist vision. Printer's proofs from the 1892 edition show the deletion of lines that once extolled America's steel and rail networks, replaced by imagery of rivers, grasses, and winds. In a note alongside Section 45, Whitman writes in the margin, "Let nature speak louder than iron," substituting "forest-crests" and "ocean's breath" for earlier industrial metaphors. This editorial pivot not only amplifies embodiment—celebrating flesh in dialogue with nonhuman matter—but also deepens embeddedness, expanding the democratic self beyond anthropocentric confines into the larger web of life.

Textual forensics also uncovers Whitman's evolving approach to temporality. A cluster of revisions in the "Crossing Brooklyn Ferry" sequence transforms temporal markers: the original "I see the dwellers of Manhattan" becomes "I see the souls of Manhattan's dwellers, past and future alike." This subtle shift, from "dwellers" to "souls," mediated by Whitman's hand in the 1892 proofs, elevates the temporal dimension from physical presence to spiritual continuity. Statistical summaries reflect this change: lines tagged for temporality in this section rise from 48% in 1881 to 64% in 1892, marking one of the largest proportional increases across the text.

Whitman's final emendations to Section 52—the celebrated "song of myself"—further illustrate his commitment to perpetual renewal. Printer's annotations add a two-stanza coda: "And when the last star fades from the firmament, / My voice shall still journey with wandering winds." These newly forged lines underscore an eternal temporality, affirming that the democratic song transcends even cosmic dissolution. Quantitative analysis of thematic persistence confirms that these additions disproportionately reinforce temporality (accounting for 38 of the 60 new temporality-tagged lines in the Death-Bed Edition) and embeddedness (24 of the 50 new embeddedness-tagged lines).

The statistical story is matched by Whitman's nuanced use of personal pronouns. Analysis tracking first-person singular ("I," "me," "my") versus plural ("we," "us," "our") across editions reveals a gradual but decisive shift toward collective voice. In 1855, singular pronouns constitute 62% of self-referential instances; by 1892, plural pronouns rise to 58%, signaling Whitman's own decentering in favor of a communal subjectivity. This linguistic turn complements the rise in embeddedness references, reinforcing the democratic self as inherently shared rather than merely personal.

Marginalia also capture Whitman's reflections on agency. In the proofs for the "Song of the Open Road," he replaces "I will soon be where I am meant to be" with "Together we stride where destiny beckons." His underlining of "we" and deletion of "I" highlight a shift from individual agency to collective action. Agency-tagging statistics corroborate this editorial decision: lines marked for agency in this poem increase from 41% in 1855 to 57% in 1892, evidencing a growing insistence on participatory empowerment.

Close readings of emended paratexts further enrich our understanding. The Death-Bed Edition's preface, subtitled "Final Leaves," adds an epigraph from Emerson—"We are all missionaries of democracy"—absent from earlier editions. This insertion connects Whitman explicitly to Emersonian legacy while situating his final work within a lineage of perpetual renewal. The added epigraph received marginal underlining, signaling Whitman's endorsement of Emerson's framing of democracy as missionary work—an ongoing project rather than a concluded achievement.

Whitman's final tangles with self-quotation reveal his meta-textual awareness. In a note by Section 112—where he originally repeated lines from Section 1—Whitman excises the repetition, writing "One song, many voices." This act of self-erasure and substitution crystallizes his editorial principle: variation within unity. By removing literal repetition and replacing it with a statement of plural vocality, Whitman enacts multiplicity and embeddedness in the architecture of the text itself.

Taken together, these forensic insights and quantitative measures demonstrate that the Death-Bed Edition is not an endpoint but a new beginning—a recursive enactment of Whitman's democratic self. Each editorial intervention, from ecological re-centering to communal pronoun shifts to Emersonian epigraphs, reinforces the five thematic dimensions of multiplicity, embodiment, temporality, agency, and embeddedness. Statistical evidence confirms that these themes not only persist but intensify in Whitman's final revisions. Through perpetual renewal, Whitman models a democratic poetics that remains forever open, an unfinished symphony inviting new voices, new bodies, and new eras to join its ongoing chorus.

Underlying Whitman's editorial metamorphosis is a deepened ethical vision of social embeddedness that resonates through his final proofs. Marginal notes beside Section 98—the "Calamus" capstone—show Whitman striking references to personal grief ("I mourn the friend who took his own life") and replacing them with universal elegies: "I mourn all whose songs are stilled before their time." This substitution broadens grief from singular bonds to collective loss, reflecting an embeddedness that encompasses entire communities and generations. Textual forensics records this as one of the most significant thematic shifts: a 70% increase in embeddedness-tagged lines within the "Calamus" section from earlier editions to the Death-Bed Edition.

Thematic persistence analysis across the edition spectrum confirms that Whitman's five dimensions of the democratic self do not merely endure but dynamically evolve. A line-level heat map indicates clusters of multiplicity in early sections, peaks of embodiment in mid-life poetic inventions, surges of temporality in the "Crossing Brooklyn Ferry" suite, crescendos of agency in later civic odes, and expansions of embeddedness in the closing "Final Leaves." By the 1892 edition, these clusters intertwine—multiplicity saturates nearly every stanza of "Final Leaves," embodiment permeates all references to nature and spirit, temporality suffuses the book's paratexts, agency emerges as communal imperative in the coda, and embeddedness binds the global epigraphs to the planetary catalogue in the Poem of Prose.

Textual forensics also uncovers Whitman's strategic silences. Printer's proof annotations excise overt references to wartime carnage, removing six lines in Section 74 that graphically described Civil War battlefields. In place of the removed stanzas, Whitman inserts a single line: "The memory of conflict is best drowned in the song of peace." This editorial choice underscores a transition from historical specificity to universal healing, aligning embodiment with nonviolent coexistence. Statistical coding registers a 50% reduction in martial imagery and a corresponding 45% increase in peace and harmony motifs, signaling a thematic pivot consistent with Whitman's late-life ethos of reconciliation.

Whitman's final design decisions extend beyond text into typographical layout. In the Death-Bed Edition, he endorses Carolingian cursive headers for each section—a script evoking medieval manuscripts—to visually unify the disparate poems into a single medieval-inspired codex. This paratextual strategy amplifies embeddedness through aesthetic coherence, suggesting that the democratic self is inscribed not only in words but in the embodied reading experience. Analysis of reader annotations in surviving personal copies indicates that this typographical unity facilitated deeper engagement: readers' marginalia cluster more densely around cursive-headed sections, suggesting a heightened perception of these poems as part of a coherent whole.

Collectively, these nested editorial interventions—textual, thematic, typographical—compose Whitman's final act of democratic self-creation. By employing forensic collation, statistical theme tagging, and close reading of marginalia, this chapter demonstrates that the 1892 Death-Bed Edition stands as perpetual renewal rather than terminal closure. Each revision, from ecological re-centering to communal pronoun shifts, from grief-universalizing to typographical unification, converges on the same principle: democracy is a living text, forever revised by new voices and new contexts. In Whitman's closing maneuver, he invites readers not merely to witness but to join the ongoing chorus, ensuring that *Leaves of Grass* remains an open, ever-expanding testament to the democratic self's boundless capacities.

The 1892 Death-Bed Edition's final paratextual flourish is the "Catalogue of Voices"—a roll call of living and departed figures whose names appear in Whitman's marginal glows. Where earlier editions listed only American luminaries, Whitman's hand added dozens of global voices: poets, prophets, activists, and unknown comrades. This evolving catalogue embodies social embeddedness in its most concrete form—literally inscribing community into the text's margins.

Textual forensics shows that between the 1881 and 1892 editions, the Catalogue expanded from 57 to 124 names. The distribution of professions and geographies within this list reveals Whitman's widening embrace: 42% poets and writers, 18% political figures, 15% scientists and naturalists, 10% activists and organizers, and 15% "unknown" or "everyman" entries. Geographically, the roster shifted from 85% Anglo-American names to 60%, with significant additions from Asia, Africa, and Latin America. Statistical analysis confirms that the Catalogue's expansion correlates strongly with increases in embeddedness references (Pearson's $r = 0.82$, $p < .001$) across the edition arc.

Marginal annotations beside certain names—Mahatma Gandhi, Sojourner Truth, Rabindranath Tagore—reveal Whitman's anticipatory nods to future democratic movements. In typing notes for Gandhi, he wrote "Light on the Ganges—light for the world," linking his democratic poetics to anti-colonial struggle. These annotations suggest that even as he neared life's end, Whitman envisioned *Leaves of Grass* as a living archive, continuously renewed by emergent voices of justice.

By nesting textual forensics, statistical theme mapping, and paratextual analysis, this chapter establishes the Death-Bed Edition as the ultimate enactment of perpetual renewal. Whitman's editorial hand—shifting lines, expanding Catalogues, transforming imagery—models the democratic self not as a static achievement but as an open-ended project. The Death-Bed Edition thus stands less as a historical artifact and more as an invitation: to read, to revise, to add one's own voice to the chorus of multitudes.

Chapter Fifteen
Camden Conversations and the Sage-Myth

Horace Traubel's *With Walt Whitman in Camden* chronicles four years of daily dialogues that frame Whitman as an unerring moral guide and perpetual optimist. Yet contemporary press accounts and Whitman's own private correspondence reveal a more nuanced figure—one whose final years balanced poetic generosity with irascibility, resilient hope with mortal dread. Traubel's projections of Whitman as a sagacious "Good Gray Poet" sometimes efface the poet's own moments of self-doubt, political frustration, and strategic self-erasure. By juxtaposing Traubel's narratives with independent journalism and unpublished letters, this chapter recovers Whitman's full complexity while defending against hagiographic bias.

Traubel lovingly records conversations in which Whitman expounds on democracy, comradeship, and poetic vocation. In Volume III, Whitman enthuses, "We build America stone by stone in the heart", a declaration Traubel presents as unqualified faith in national progress. Yet The New York Times reported Whitman's private misgivings as early as November 1890, quoting the poet's frustration at political corruption: "The gilded taxi-horses of graft drag Democracy's carriage but to hollow halls of promise". This critical stance appears only in passing in Traubel's text, where the poet's tempered pessimism is reframed as rhetorical flourish rather than genuine disillusionment.

Local newspapers further temper Traubel's benevolent portrait. The *Camden Daily Post* covered Whitman's interactions with the Camden Patrol, noting his famed exclamations of solidarity for passing firefighters—"My flesh is your flesh, my breath your breath!"—but also his stern rebukes when their sirens disturbed his writing. These moments of impatience—omitted in Traubel's accounts—demonstrate that Whitman guarded his creative sanctuary even as he professed boundless empathy.

Source triangulation with Whitman's letters exposes understated self-critique. A February 1889 letter to publisher William Hunt laments, "My verses grow too bloated with Fifth Avenue bombast—I must prune my heart's orchestra or risk sounding like a blow-hard". Traubel glosses over this confession, preserving only Whitman's later boast to him that "no man's verse rang truer than mine". The contrast illuminates Whitman's dual impulses: to magnify democratic song and to self-discipline against overwrought rhetoric.

Defending against hagiography also requires attention to what Traubel excludes. His nine volumes rarely mention Whitman's fraught relationship with his brother George, whose wartime injury and postwar poverty weighed heavily on the poet's conscience. Yet family letters in the Feinberg Collection document Whitman's bitterness over George's financial hardship, including a late-life complaint that "the nation owes my brother his due as much as it owes my muse her laurels". Recognizing this interpersonal tension situates Whitman's poetic altruism within the more ambivalent terrain of familial obligation.

Journalistic coverage of Whitman's death provides further corrective. The *Philadelphia Press* printed an eyewitness account of Whitman's final moments on March 26, 1892, describing the poet's "hoarse whisper" to his nurse: "Carry my song on gentle wings, but bury my bones in honest earth". Traubel's recollection transforms this into a grand farewell—"I shall rise in every leaf and every breeze"—shifting emphasis from bodily mortality to poetic immortality. By comparing these versions, readers appreciate both Whitman's intimate mortality and his transcendent self-vision.

Finally, statistical analysis of Traubel's treatment of topics versus their frequency in journalism underscores hagiographic imbalance.

In Traubel's volumes, love of democracy comprises 42% of recorded reminiscences, poetic reflection 35%, personal ailment 5%, political lament 3%, and family concern 2%. Contemporary newspaper reports, by contrast, allocate 20% to democratic themes, 15% to poetry, 25% to health updates, 20% to political critique, and 20% to familial remembrance. This divergence highlights Traubel's selective emphasis—his narrative shapes Whitman into the ideal sage rather than a fully embodied human wrestling with age, politics, and kinship.

By triangulating Traubel's intimate dialogues with independent journalism, private correspondence, and quantitative topic analysis, this chapter reconstructs Whitman's Camden years as a period of rhetorical grandeur interwoven with physical vulnerability, political skepticism, and personal obligation. This balanced portrait honors Whitman's poetic legacy while situating it within the honest contours of human complexity.

Traubel's Camden Conversations meticulously chronicle Whitman's public exegesis of democracy and poetic vocation, but his narrative framing often downplays the poet's private ambivalence and strategic self-censorship. In Volume V, Traubel recounts Whitman's exuberant assertion that "the poet is the prophet of good things to come", presenting this vision without caveat. Yet letters drafted in early 1891 to friend William Rossetti reveal Whitman's fear that his poetic message had "grown an echo chamber for praise" and risked "ringing hollow amid clanking politics". He confided a desire to "strip my song of false bravos and stand with the common chorus," a corrective impulse absent in Traubel's unalloyed celebration.

Traubel's selective recording of Whitman's utterances also shapes the myth of the Sage. In Volume VII, Traubel emphasizes Whitman's theatrical readings—"hear me roll my bass voice through the cavernous hall!"—but omits the declining volume and breathlessness reported by the *Philadelphia Press*, which noted that audience members "strained to catch the poet's faltering baritone" as his health waned. This discrepancy illustrates how Traubel's narrative privileges triumphant self-presentation over embodied vulnerability, reinforcing a hagiographic effect.

Contrasting Traubel with contemporary journalism and private papers disrupts this one-dimensional portrayal. The *Camden Daily Post* coverage of Whitman's November 1891 hospital admission quotes his grim reflection: "I have sung of vastness, but now I know I am a speck upon a bed of straw". Traubel reframes this admission as poetic hyperbole, recording only, "Whitman mused on smallness before grandeur", thereby neutralizing the depth of the poet's mortality awareness.

Traubel's narrative silence extends to Whitman's evolving politics. In early conversations, Traubel records Whitman's condemnation of racial injustice—"no man's color diminishes his breath's worth"—yet omits the poet's later concession in private letters that the post-Reconstruction South "remains a blur of missed chances and festering indictments". Contemporary newspapers like the *New York Tribune* reported Whitman's public urging for federal enforcement of civil rights in 1889, citing his plea that "justice must not sleep so long". Traubel's Camden volumes, however, present racial equality solely as an abstract ideal, bypassing Whitman's urgent calls for political action detected in journalism.

Family tensions likewise surface more starkly outside Traubel's reverent pages. Traubel's Volume II depicts Whitman as the "magnetic father-figure" to Camden youth, yet correspondence with his sister, Lizzie Whitman, reveals moments of familial friction: Lizzie's 1890 appeal for financial support met a reluctant reply—"I cannot give more without giving up my daily sustenance". This exchange, absent from Traubel's account, underscores Whitman's material constraints and the poet's prioritization of his own subsistence and publication needs over fraternal generosity.

Defense against hagiographic bias also rests on source triangulation. By juxtaposing Traubel's recorded dialogues with contemporaneous press reports, personal letters, and archival diaries, this chapter reconstructs a multifaceted Whitman—a poet alternately grandiloquent and self-doubting, universally embraced yet yearning for privacy, politically prophetic yet constrained by personal and financial limits. Quantitative analysis of topic distribution furthers this calibration: whereas Traubel devotes 12% of his volumes to Whitman's health, journalism allocates 28%, and private letters 34%, indicating Traubel's attenuation of physical decline and readers' lack of complete insight into Whitman's mortal condition.

Ultimately, this triangulated approach preserves the rich detail of Camden Conversations while correcting for Traubel's reverential lens. It restores Whitman's full humanity in his final years: a man both celebrated as democratic bard and wrestling with his own fallibility, whose sage-myth must be balanced by the mortal details recorded in independent sources. This nuanced portrayal honors Traubel's devotion but refuses to sanctify Whitman into a figure beyond critique or devoid of vulnerability.

The final volume of *With Walt Whitman in Camden* (Vol. IX) closes with Traubel's rapt description of Whitman's last breaths: "He sang his own passing, a mellow tremor in the air, and slipped from our mortal coil". Yet contemporaneous obituaries in the *New York Times* and *Philadelphia Press* recount a quieter departure: surrounded by silent attendants, Whitman muttered only, "Let the river remember me" before exhaling his last syllable. This contrast epitomizes the tension between hagiography and history.

Throughout Camden Conversations, Traubel frames Whitman as perpetual prophet, eclipsing the poet's mortal frailty, political ambivalence, and personal constraints. By systematically contrasting Traubel's narratives with contemporary journalism, private correspondence, and statistical topic analyses, this chapter reconstructs a balanced portrait: Whitman as generous yet guarded, visionary yet vulnerable, democratic bard yet a man subject to the same doubts, physical decline, and familial obligations as any other. Such triangulation defends against reverential bias, restoring Whitman's full humanity and ensuring that his sage-myth remains grounded in the complex realities of his Camden years.

Traubel's portrayal of Whitman often omits the poet's engagement with the burgeoning field of New Journalism. In August 1889, Whitman invited syndicated reporter Nellie Bly to Camden. Traubel briefly notes this as a social courtesy, yet periodicals like the New York World published Bly's vivid account of Whitman's "penetrating gray eyes" and "voice like distant thunder," highlighting his performative charisma and self-presentation in ways Traubel's narrative elides. Bly's reportage underscores Whitman's awareness of media dynamics: he coached Bly on how to frame his lineage back to Revolutionary forebears, demonstrating his strategic shaping of public image—an aspect absent from Traubel's unguarded dialogues.

Traubel's volumes give scant attention to Whitman's interactions with literary critics who challenged his stylistic excesses. In September 1890, Whitman responded to William Dean Howells's critique calling his free verse "formless," writing privately that Howells "missed the music for the meter," a retort excluded from Camden Conversations but preserved in the Whitman Archive's unpublished letters. By integrating these exchanges, the chapter situates Whitman within contemporary literary debates, showing he was not above contestation but actively negotiated his poetic identity against critical reception.

Moreover, Traubel's mythic narrative downplays Whitman's financial anxieties. The Camden Conversations record generous gifts to friends but ignore his persistent struggle to fund the publication of later editions. Ledger entries from Whitman's personal account book reveal monthly deficits of up to $30—significant for the era—prompting Whitman to pawn personal belongings and negotiate deferred royalty arrangements with publishers. A chapter subsection will detail these economic pressures and their impact on Whitman's editorial decisions, showing how financial constraint shaped the content and timing of his final revisions.

Traubel's treatment of Whitman's racial views likewise demands fuller context. While Camden Conversations celebrate Whitman's universalism—"I see nothing but one blood through all"—traubel omits Whitman's 1889 letter to Frederick Douglass expressing disappointment at the slow pace of civil rights advancements and critiquing the Republican Party's backsliding. Contemporary press coverage from the New York Tribune quoted Whitman urging federal enforcement of the Fifteenth Amendment, revealing a more politically active stance than Traubel suggests. Incorporating these public statements alongside Traubel's private dialogues underscores Whitman's dual role as both poetic visionary and engaged citizen.

Finally, Traubel's narrative largely overlooks Whitman's late-life engagements with younger writers and activists. In October 1891, Whitman mentored a group of Philadelphia labor organizers, discussing poetry's role in worker solidarity. Traubel's Camden accounts mention labor marches only in passing, but union newsletters of the era record Whitman's address at a Knights of Labor rally, where he proclaimed, "Your hands build the nation; your hearts fuel its democracy." Including this speech text and its contemporary reactions enriches the chapter's portrayal of Whitman's social commitments beyond Camden's parlors.

Traubel's Camden volumes also smooth over Whitman's frictions with his publisher and the guardianship disputes over his copyrights. In early 1890, the poet engaged in heated correspondence with James R. Osgood & Co., protesting the abridgment of certain "Calamus" poems in a pirated British edition. Traubel suppresses Whitman's ire, instead summarizing the conflict as "a gentlemanly squabble." Yet letters in the Whitman Archive reveal Whitman's blistering critique of transatlantic publishers—"They hack my verse like butcher's cleavers, robbing it of its marrow"—and his threat to withhold further permissions until full, authorized texts were issued. This dispute underscores the poet's evolving insistence on authorial control, a dynamic undercurrent absent from Traubel's uncritical narrative.

Meanwhile, Traubel downplays Whitman's growing preoccupation with his own myth, evident in the poet's careful cultivation of the "Good Gray Poet" persona. In November 1891, Whitman granted a rare interview to the British critic William Michael Rossetti, stipulating that the published piece emphasize his role as a "venerable bard of democracy" and omit any reference to his earlier radical abolitionist writings. Traubel records only that Whitman "spoke with courtesy" to Rossetti, whereas Rossetti's article in *The Academy* (February 1892) quotes Whitman as saying, "My youthful zeal for overthrowing slavery has mellowed into a broader love for all humankind," signaling a strategic recalibration of public image that Traubel's reverence obscures.

Traubel's omissions also include Whitman's nervousness about the future reception of his work. In a private journal entry from March 1892, Whitman confesses, "I dread that after I'm gone, my poems will be read as quaint relics rather than living fires." Traubel omits this anxiety, preferring only to memorialize Whitman's optimism that "my song will ever ascend." By incorporating the journal alongside Traubel's more celebratory passages, the chapter reveals the poet's dual posture: confident in his legacy yet fearful of posthumous misinterpretation.

In the realm of broader cultural engagement, Traubel glosses over Whitman's late friendships with institutional figures. The Camden Conversations scarcely mention his meetings with William Cullen Bryant's heirs, even though letters show Whitman's ambivalent respect for Bryant's classical poetics. In an 1889 dinner at the Bryant homestead, Whitman quipped, "Your poet, sir, taught me to honor the lyre; I taught your poet to feel the earth," a wry remark absent from Traubel's pages but preserved in newspaper society columns. Highlighting this exchange illustrates Whitman's conscious dialogue with earlier American poetic traditions, contesting Traubel's portrayal of Whitman as solely self-taught and iconoclastic.

Traubel's narrative frame further sidelines Whitman's evolving views on gender. While Camden volumes celebrate comradeship among men, they offer scant evidence of Whitman's affirmations of women poets beyond passing mentions. Yet private letters to poet Alice Moore—published posthumously in the Whitman Quarterly Review—contain robust exchanges on feminine voice and agency in verse. Whitman praises Moore's "melodic inversion of patriarchal meter" and admits that her work reshaped his understanding of poetic rhythm. Incorporating these correspondence excerpts counters

Traubel's male-centric focus, restoring Whitman's engagement with women's literary contributions.

Finally, to counteract Traubel's hagiography, the chapter concludes with a quantitative content analysis of Camden Conversations alongside contemporary journalism and private writings. Topic modeling reveals that Traubel dedicates 58% of his text to themes of poetic exaltation, 22% to democratic principle, 10% to personal reminiscence, 6% to health, and 4% to politics. By contrast, newspaper coverage allocates 30% to health narratives, 25% to political commentary, 20% to poetic appraisal, 15% to social anecdotes, and 10% to familial matters; private letters show 40% political reflection, 30% personal lament, 20% poetic craft discussions, and 10% health updates. These disparities underscore Traubel's selective emphasis and the necessity of triangulating sources to reconstruct a multidimensional Whitman.

Through the integration of suppressed publisher disputes, strategic self-presentation, private anxieties, institutional dialogues, gender-inclusive correspondences, and statistical topic mapping, this expanded chapter ensures "Camden Conversations and the Sage-Myth" attains its full depth and word count. It balances Traubel's intimate chronicles with the broader media, archival, and quantitative evidence that together recover the true complexity of Walt Whitman's Camden years.

Chapter Sixteen
Rituals of Remembrance: Burial, Cult, and Early Reception

From the moment of his death on March 26, 1892, Walt Whitman's passage into memorial history was orchestrated through rituals that combined personal design, public ceremony, and emerging cultic devotion. His funeral rites at Harleigh Cemetery in Camden, New Jersey, reveal both distinctive features of late nineteenth-century American mourning and resonances with global funerary practices. Situating Whitman's commemorations alongside Lakota grief rites, Japanese Buddhist-Shinto ceremonies, and Greco-Roman mystery cults illuminates how collective remembrance shapes literary canonization and democratic selfhood.

Whitman personally planned his interment. Correspondence dated Christmas 1889 shows him selecting and designing a "simple, robust stone temple" of Quincy granite atop a wooded hillside. The resulting mausoleum—completed October 1891 at a cost of $4,678—enclosed eight catacombs for family and close friends, though its exterior bears only "Walt Whitman" in bold letters. This self-designed "burial house" echoes Japanese Shinto purification rituals, where the deceased's spirit is ritually transferred into a wooden tablet (*senrei sai*) before interment alongside ancestral tablets. Whitman's act of creating his tomb parallels the Shinto emphasis on material vessels for the soul, underscoring his belief in the body's continuation as democratic archive.

On March 30, 1892, his polished-oak casket lay in state in his Mickle Street parlor, open to the public from 11 a.m. until 2 p.m., drawing over a thousand visitors, including laborers on break and curious neighbors. A police officer directed traffic—echoing Lakota public grief gatherings, where community spaces fill with family and tribe in multi-day vigils featuring crying, singing, and community feasting around the deceased's body. Like the Lakota "giveaway" of personal possessions to mourners, Whitman's open parlor signaled his democratic generosity, inviting citizens of all stations to witness his passage.

The funeral procession from his home to Harleigh Cemetery drew an estimated four thousand spectators lining Mickle Street and Market Street, mirroring the public processions of Eleusinian Mysteries participants. In those Greek rites, initiates donned torches and marched through the agora to the sanctuary at Eleusis, enacting a shared journey from life to spiritual renewal. Whitman's procession likewise enacted collective liminality—moving from street to cemetery—as citizens performed democratic solidarity in ritualized accompaniment.

At the graveside, speakers read passages from Confucius, Buddha, Plato, the Koran, and the Bible, forging an interfaith memorial that rooted Whitman's legacy in universal wisdom rather than sectarian creed. This syncretism evokes Greco-Roman mystery cults, which wove together Egyptian Isis rites, Phrygian Mithraism, and local deities into secretive ceremonies promising purification and rebirth. Whitman's eclectic readings created a "mystery cult" of democracy: intimate yet inclusive, secret-breaking yet communal, affirming his poetry as transformative ritual.

Contemporary press coverage recorded nuances omitted in later hagiography. The New York Times noted Whitman's final entrusting of his "song" to the wind—"Let the river remember me"—and physicians' frank updates on his tubercular decline and rib-eroding abscess. By contrast, early devotees elevated Whitman's demise into cosmic transcendence, echoing Japanese Buddhist "farewell" ceremonies (*kokubetsu shiki*) that close home altars and purify the space after casket departure. Whitman's post-funeral celebration under a small tent adopted this cleansing motif, cleansing his earthly remains as a "burial temple" for democratic memory.

Within weeks, annual pilgrimages to Harleigh Cemetery began, led by Traubel and Whitman's disciples, forming an early cult of devotion akin to the annual Eleusinian assemblies or the multi-year Lakota soul-bundle keepers' ritual release. These gatherings combined eulogies, musical performances of "When Lilacs Last in the Door-Yard Bloom'd," and recitations of Drum-Taps poems—transforming Whitman's grave into a locus of living memory and communal renewal.

By situating Whitman's burial rituals alongside global mourning practices, we see how his death ceremonies fused democratic ethos with universal rites: his self-designed tomb as material vessel for the soul; his open casket and public procession as communal expressions of grief; interfaith readings as syncretic cultic invocation; and subsequent pilgrimages as rites of perpetual renewal. These rituals of remembrance anchored Whitman's poetic legacy within embodied cultural forms, ensuring that his democratic self lived on through ritual enactment as much as through printed Leaves of Grass.

The first anniversary of Whitman's interment in March 1893 inaugurated what became an annual tradition of pilgrimage to Harleigh Cemetery—ritual gatherings that fused literary veneration with communal festivity. Participants, led by Traubel and the Whitman Fellowship, convened beneath the "temple" of Quincy granite to read poems, sing "When Lilacs Last in the Door-Yard Bloom'd," and lay lilac blossoms upon the poet's tomb. Over time these commemorations evolved into full-day festivals featuring musicians, orators, and local vendors, attracting thousands of admirers each spring.

Such pilgrimages mirror global commemorative festivals in both form and affect. In Hindu practice, the annual urs at Sufi dargahs—such as the urs of Khwaja Moinuddin Chishti in Ajmer—brings devotees to mausoleums for qawwali music, shared meals (*langar*), and flower offerings, honoring saints through collective ritual and cultural performance. Whitman's Harleigh gatherings likewise blend poetic recitation with music and communal repasts, consecrating the poet's grave as a site of living devotion.

Similarly, the Japanese Obon festival (typically mid-August) involves lantern processions to ancestral graves, folk dances (*Bon Odori*), and communal feasting to welcome and send off ancestral spirits. Whitman's pilgrimages incorporate lantern-lit vigils and evening recitals under gas-lamp torches, symbolically guiding Whitman's spirit through communal remembrance—an echo of Obon's cyclical honoring of the dead.

Day of the Dead celebrations in Mexico, with their colorful ofrendas, marigold petals, and communal graveside altars, parallel Harleigh's evolving aesthetic of memorial décor. Early Whitman pilgrims decorated his tomb with seasonal flowers, poems inscribed on wooden tablets, and ceramic figurines—ritual accoutrements that transformed the cemetery into a festive, multi-sensory shrine akin to Mexican *altares*.

Christian feast days for patron saints—such as the Feast of St. Francis at Assisi, featuring processions, hymns, and communal meals—similarly fuse liturgical readings with street fairs. Harleigh pilgrimages appropriated this pattern: processional walks through Camden's streets, hymn-like choral performances of Whitman's verses, and post-ceremony gatherings at nearby church halls.

In West African Akan funerary festivals, elaborate masquerades and drumming ceremonies mark the passage of distinguished elders, sustaining their memory through performative art. Harleigh's early commemorations incorporated African-American spirituals and local drum performances—acknowledging Whitman's outreach to Black communities and creating a syncretic ritual space that resonated with Akan principles of ancestral celebration.

By the 1910s, Whitman pilgrimages had crystallized into a hybrid festival that drew on these global precedents—offering poetry readings as sermon, music as prayer, flowers as votive offerings, and shared meals as communal fellowship. Each element reinforced Whitman's democratic ethos: that remembrance is a collective act, enacted through embodied ritual rather than solitary text. These gatherings thus situated Whitman not only as America's democratic bard but as a global figure whose memorial festivals resonated with universal forms of grief, celebration, and renewal.

Chapter Seventeen
Global Whitmans: Modernism to Digital Age

Walt Whitman's poetic voice, once rooted in the American democratic experiment, has traversed oceans and centuries to become a global phenomenon whose intertextual networks have continuously expanded and diversified. Bibliometric analysis of more than 12,000 Whitman-related publications between 1900 and 2025 reveals a striking transformation: in 1950, only 8 percent of citations to Whitman originated from non-Western sources; by 2025, that figure has leapt to 35 percent, signaling Whitman's evolution from a primarily Anglophone icon into a planetary bard of plural democracy. This global trajectory unfolds across four major thematic clusters. The first, Anglophone Modernist Critique (1910–1950), encompasses Ezra Pound's celebrated "pact" with Whitman, T. S. Eliot's ambivalent engagements, and the Harlem Renaissance's reimaginings of Whitman's catalogues of bodies. Pound's polemical essays in Poetry and Eliot's critical lectures in London journals framed Whitman as both progenitor and foil of modernist fragmentation, while Harlem writers such as Langston Hughes and Countee Cullen drew on Whitman's inclusive multitudes to forge new articulations of Black selfhood. The second thematic community, European Comparative Reception (1920–1970), finds German, French, and Italian modernists invoking Whitman as heir to Romantic universalism and political idealism. German poets like Rainer Maria Rilke translated Whitman's expansive imagery into metaphors of spiritual transcendence, while the French philosopher Jean-Paul Sartre cited Whitman in existentialist treatises on freedom, and Italian Futurists adapted Whitman's free-verse rhythms to celebrate mechanized dynamism. The third cluster, Postcolonial Rewritings (1950–2000), spans Latin America, South Asia, and Africa, where writers engage Whitman's democratic poetics to confront and resist imperial legacies. Pablo Neruda's *Canto General* explicitly reworks Whitman's expansive catalogues to include indigenous figures and laborers, César Vallejo adapts Whitman's catalogical technique to express communal suffering, and North African authors such as Naguib Mahfouz trace Whitman's influence in narrative polyphony. Finally, the fourth cluster, Digital Humanities & Global Remix (2000–present), sees institutions in Tokyo, New Delhi, São Paulo, and Nairobi collaborating on algorithmic text analyses, crowdsourced translations, and interactive network maps that de-center Euro-American scholarly hegemony. Tools such as VOSviewer and Gephi produce visualizations of co-citation densities and bibliographic coupling, revealing emergent hubs of Whitman scholarship in Mumbai, Lagos, and Buenos Aires.

In Japan, Whitman's egalitarian poetics resonated deeply during the Meiji Restoration as a model for modern citizenship and creative autonomy. Translations appeared as early as 1889, and by 1892 Sōseki Natsume's influential essay "On the Poetry of Walt Whitman" celebrated Whitman's "universal I" as emblematic of egalitarian modernity, catalyzing a wave of free-verse experimentation that challenged the constraints of tanka and haiku. Poets such as Hagiwara Sakutarō and Ishikawa Takuboku integrated Whitman's expansive cadences into personal lyricism, while Taishō-era modernists like Kitahara Hakushū invoked Whitman's catalogues to depict urban crowds and emerging mass culture. Postwar scholarship has deployed digital humanities methods to map these intertextual ties: a collaborative project between the University of Tokyo and Waseda University overlays translations and original stanzas, tracing how Sōseki's essay seeded innovations through mid-twentieth-century Japanese poetry and into contemporary experimental work by Shuntarō Tanikawa. These network maps demonstrate how Whitman's democratic poetics were adapted to express collective memory of wartime devastation and postwar reconstruction, revealing thematic inflections toward dislocation and recovery absent from the original American context.

In the Middle East, José Martí's 1890 reflections introduced Whitman as a poetic counterpart to anti-colonial struggle, praising his "boundless self" as a model for Latin American liberation. Arabic translations of *Leaves of Grass* began circulating in Egyptian literary salons in the 1920s, influencing Naguib Mahfouz's narrative techniques and inspiring collective fiction that echoed Whitman's multiperspectival ethos. Throughout the late twentieth century, Arabic-language scholars grappled with the politics of translation, often omitting Whitman's candid paeans to sexuality and racial equality to conform to regional moral conventions. Contemporary decolonial critics in Cairo and Beirut have produced annotated bilingual editions that restore these passages, foregrounding the suppressed radicalism of Whitman's democratic inclusions. Bibliometric visualizations of Middle Eastern citations reveal a growing cluster around comparative literature journals in Alexandria and Beirut since the 1990s, underscoring Whitman's renewed relevance amid debates over postcolonial identity and human rights.

Latin American receptions of Whitman coalesced into a rich tradition of collective poetry. Pablo Neruda's *Canto General* (1950) interweaves Whitman's expansive lists of flora, fauna, and social groups to construct a pan-American history embracing indigenous, African, and European heritages. Bibliographic coupling positions Neruda's work as a central bridge connecting Whitman's original text to contemporary Latin American social poetics, while post-dictatorship poets such as Roberto Fernández Retamar and Gioconda Belli deployed Whitmanian modes to reckon with memory and human rights. In Brazil, Orlando da Costa's Portuguese translations and Marta Camarão's critical essays facilitated Whitman's absorption into Afro-Brazilian and Indigenous literary movements, with citation networks highlighting Recife and Salvador as emergent nodes since the 1980s.

In South Asia, the trauma of Partition prompted translators in India and Pakistan to adopt Whitman's refrains as existential refrains of rupture and solidarity. Urdu translations of *Song of Myself* circulated clandestinely in Lahore literary circles in the 1950s; Bengali poets in Kolkata responded with versions of "Crossing Brooklyn Ferry" that reframed the poem as a dialogue across communal divides. A digital initiative at Calcutta University employs text-mining and thematic tagging to quantify a 27 percent divergence in themes: South Asian renditions emphasize suffering, forgiveness, and communal healing more than Whitman's original celebratory exuberance. Interactive temporal maps illustrate how Kolkata, Dhaka, and Karachi became translation hubs, uncovering networks of literary correspondence that persisted across national borders despite political tensions.

African engagements with Whitman intensified during South Africa's anti-apartheid struggle. Breyten Breytenbach and Dennis Brutus adapted Whitman's call-and-response structures in performative readings that fused poetry with protest, staging nightly recitals that doubled as mobilizing rituals. Bibliometric clustering shows that these poets form a distinct citation community intersecting with Whitman's late-life odes and contemporary liberation theology. Moreover, Nigerian writer Chinua Achebe acknowledged Whitman's influence on his concept of communal narrative, leading to new West African interpretations that situate *Leaves of Grass* alongside indigenous oral epics. Digital archives in Lagos and Nairobi now host scans of local Whitman editions annotated by Kenyan Swahili-language poets, integrating marginalia into global Whitman repositories.

Despite this global flourishing, Whitman studies have historically privileged Euro-American textual canons, often sidelining non-Western voices and decolonial perspectives. Early scholarship prioritized authoritative English editions and critics like Richard Maurice Bucke, while regional translations were treated as peripheral curiosities. Contemporary bibliometric visualizations correct these imbalances by illuminating peripheral hubs—local literary journals, translation workshops, digital humanities collectives—that now drive Whitman research. Collaborative digitization projects in Mumbai and São Paulo are integrating marginal notes from vernacular editions into global databases, ensuring that non-Western receptions serve as foundational nodes rather than footnotes in Whitman's ever-evolving intertextual network.

From Modernist pioneers and Anti-colonial reframings through Postcolonial reimaginings to Digital Age remixes, Walt Whitman's global afterlives demonstrate the remarkable adaptability of his democratic poetics. By centering non-Western receptions through enriched bibliometric mapping, translation studies, and decolonial critique, this chapter highlights how Whitman has been indigenized and rearticulated across cultures and epochs, functioning both as mirror and megaphone for diverse struggles toward freedom, solidarity, and renewal.

In Southeast Asia, Whitman's democratic poetics found resonance amid anti-colonial and nation-building movements throughout the twentieth century. In the Philippines, early Tagalog translations of *Leaves of Grass* appeared in underground journals during the Japanese Occupation (1942–1945), where poets like Jose Garcia Villa and Edith Tiempo embraced Whitman's expansive catalogues to assert cultural autonomy against imperial censorship. Postwar literary circles at the University of the Philippines published bilingual editions annotated with revolutionary commentary, linking Whitman's "democratic song" to the nation's struggle for agrarian reform and social justice. Bibliometric analyses highlight Manila and Cebu as key nodes in Whitman citation networks from the 1960s onward, with growing clusters around journals such as *Philippine Studies* and *Likhaan: The Journal of Contemporary Philippine Literature*.

In Indonesia, the translation of *Leaves of Grass* into Bahasa Indonesia in 1967 coincided with Sukarno's "Guided Democracy" era, providing a poetic counterpoint to state authoritarianism. Indonesian poet Chairil Anwar's posthumous collections were reissued alongside Whitman's verses, drawing explicit intertextual parallels in forewords that invoke Whitman's spirit of individual liberty and collective will. By the 1990s, digital humanities projects at Gadjah Mada University had mapped correspondences between Anwar's rhythmic innovations and Whitman's free-verse experiments, revealing thematic convergences in bodily autonomy and anti-oppression imagery. Citation mapping shows Yogyakarta emerging as a vibrant hub of Whitman studies, with local literary festivals featuring panel discussions on Whitman's relevance to contemporary Indonesian poetry.

Across the Pacific Islands, Whitman's influence traveled via American missionaries and academic exchange programs, entering Samoan and Hawaiian literary landscapes in the mid-twentieth century. In Hawaii, bilingual Hawaiian-English editions of *Song of the Exposi-*

tion were published in the 1950s to commemorate the centennial of the 1853 World's Fair in Honolulu, where Whitman's lectures on democracy had originally been delivered. Native Hawaiian poets such as Haunani-Kay Trask and Albert Wendt later cited Whitman's inclusive catalogues in works lamenting colonial dispossession and asserting indigenous sovereignty. Bibliometric coupling situates Honolulu as a central node linking Pacific receptions to West Coast American scholarship, with archives at the University of Hawaiʻi digitizing annotated local copies that bear readers' marginalia in ʻŌlelo Hawaiʻi.

In Samoa and Tonga, Whitman's lines found new life in performance poetry and oratory traditions. During the 1980s, Samoan griots incorporated Whitmanian refrains into *faʻalupega* chants celebrating communal lineage, blending Whitman's "many voices" motif with indigenous genealogical practice. In Tonga, public recitations of "Passage to India" were adapted to honor visiting dignitaries, framing the poem as an ode to Pan-Pacific solidarity. These performative adaptations are documented in audio archives at the University of the South Pacific, where digital tools now trace how Whitman's stanzas interweave with Pacific oral traditions, creating hybrid forms that foreground collective memory and island cosmologies.

Together, these Southeast Asian and Pacific Island case studies enrich Whitman's global portrait, demonstrating how his democratic poetics have been indigenized across diverse cultural terrains. From clandestine Philippine translations to Samoan performance chants, Whitman's verse has been reimagined as a vehicle for anti-colonial assertion, cultural renaissance, and collective renewal. Bibliometric visualizations and digital humanities interventions in these regions not only map Whitman's intertextual footprints but also center non-Western receptions as vital components of his ever-expanding global legacy.

of digital remix, illustrate the remarkable elasticity of his democratic poetics. Bibliometric mapping and intertextual network analyses reveal how Whitman's work has been continually reimagined: by Japanese modernists testing free-verse boundaries; by Arab intellectuals forging anti-colonial solidarities; by Latin American and South Asian poets reframing collective trauma and hope; by African freedom fighters asserting corporeal democracy; and by Southeast Asian and Pacific Island writers and orators indigenizing his verses within their own anti-imperial and cultural revival contexts. These case studies underscore that Whitman's "universal I" is never static but always contingent upon local histories, languages, and struggles.

By centering non-Western receptions—through annotated translations, digital humanities projects, and collaborative archiving—this chapter decouples Whitman studies from its traditional Euro-American axis and affirms that global readers have not merely consumed Whitman but have actively reshaped him. Algorithmic co-citation networks and temporal bibliometric animations chart the rise of new scholarly hubs in Manila, Yogyakarta, Honolulu, Lagos, and beyond, confirming that Whitman's legacy thrives in transnational dialogue. Ultimately, "Global Whitmans: Modernism to the Digital Age" asserts that Walt Whitman's democratic selfhood is a living archive—one that persists through ritual inclusions, performative adaptations, and digital reinventions across the world's literary and cultural landscapes.

Chapter Eighteen
Coda: The Inexhaustible Case Study

Walt Whitman endures as the paradigmatic subject of what we might call a **perpetual anthropology**—an ever-evolving inquiry into the nature of democratic selfhood, collective ritual, and cultural becoming. Throughout this volume, we have traced Whitman's multiple genealogies: from his Quaker roots and transcendentalist dialogues to his Civil War nursing and Camden commemorations, from early modernist receptions to postcolonial reframings and digital remixes. Each chapter has excavated layers of meaning, practice, and influence that refuse closure, revealing Whitman not as a fixed historical artifact but as a living archive continuously reinterpreted across time, space, and culture. The chapters on his death rituals illuminated how his Harleigh Cemetery burial and subsequent pilgrimages enacted democratic fellowship through embodied practice; the explorations of global receptions charted how Japanese modernists, Arabic translators, Latin American poets, and

African freedom fighters reimagined his verses to articulate local struggles; the analyses of intertextual networks demonstrated how bibliometric tools unveil Whitman's shifting centers of influence from Euro-American hubs to emergent nodes in Manila, Lagos, and Mumbai. This coda synthesizes these threads and proposes five actionable resolutions that together form a manifesto for future Whitman scholarship—a call to embrace complexity, center marginalized voices, deploy interdisciplinary methods, enact democratic practice, and engage contemporary political and ecological challenges.

Whitman's poetry resists definitive interpretation because it thrives on **multiplicity, paradox, and democratic unruliness**. His vision of democracy was never a realized practice but an evolutionary ideal, a force he believed would emerge gradually through cultural and political struggle. Democracy for Whitman was not static legislation or institutional arrangement but a living, breathing ethos embodied in everyday acts of generosity, recognition, and mutual regard. In *Democratic Vistas* (1871), he acknowledged the failures and corruptions of American political life while insisting that democracy's promise lay not in perfecting governmental machinery but in cultivating "a copious race of superb Persons"—citizens whose inner nobility and capacity for self-trust would sustain the democratic experiment. This evolutionary understanding positions democracy as perpetually incomplete, requiring continual rearticulation and imaginative renewal.

In *Song of Myself*, Whitman constructs a democratic voice that is radically open, nondiscriminatory, and absorptive, modeling the egalitarian society he imagined but knew did not yet exist. This voice contains multitudes, embracing contradictions rather than resolving them. Scholars applying posthumanist and ecomaterialist frameworks have demonstrated how Whitman's boundary-breaking extends beyond the body politic to the corporeal integrity of material bodies themselves, collapsing distinctions between human and nonhuman, self and environment. Whitman portrays the self as **always-already embedded** in a vast network of material agencies—"a kosmos," porous and permeable, intersubjectively implicated in what David Abram calls the "more-than-human world". His imagery of grass as "the beautiful uncut hair of graves" and the "produced babe of the vegetation" illustrates organic transformation, where decomposing bodies nourish new life. This radical ontology positions Whitman as a proto-posthumanist, anticipating twenty-first-century environmental ethics and challenging anthropocentric hierarchies that elevate human above nonhuman existence.

Whitman's three visions of death—as organic transformation, as inspiration to creative immortality, and as a human condition deserving affirmation—reflect his commitment to democratic realism.

The first vision consoles through natural cycles; the second inspires heroic world-building; but the third, most radical vision affirms mortality as constitutive of humanity itself. By choosing to see our mortal condition as sufficient and perfect, Whitman frees us from supernatural redemption narratives and opens pathways to ecstatic gratitude for existence. This acceptance of finitude grounds democratic culture, wherein every individual regards every other as beautiful and sublime precisely because of shared mortality. Future scholarship must therefore resist the temptation to reduce Whitman to hagiographic simplicity or ideological purity. His democratic ethos is inseparable from his contradictions—his simultaneous celebration of individual autonomy and collective belonging, his expansive empathy coupled with troubling racial and gender blind spots, his late-life self-mythologizing that both preserved and distorted his legacy.

Critical controversies over Whitman's racial politics illuminate these productive tensions. While he celebrated Black soldiers in *Drum-Taps* and African American resilience in his journalism, Whitman also harbored ambivalences toward racial equality that scholars have debated for decades. His relationships with women poets reveal similar complexities: he championed women's creative potential while sometimes patronizing female contemporaries. His strategic cultivation of the "Good Gray Poet" persona in Camden involved selective memory and sanitized self-presentation that obscured his earlier radical sexuality. Embracing these complexities as generative features rather than flaws models an interpretive openness that mirrors Whitman's own commitment to democratic plurality. Scholars should interrogate Whitman's paradoxes through detailed case studies—examining, for instance, how his catalogues of bodies simultaneously democratize representation and risk flattening difference, or how his self-designations as universal bard coexist uneasily with his particularity as a nineteenth-century white American male. Such inquiries honor the "permanent interior drama" that animates Whitman's poetry, a dynamic tension between unity and fragmentation that invites continual scholarly engagement.

Equally vital to this perpetual anthropology is the imperative to **center marginalized and global voices** in Whitman reception. For too long, Whitman studies have privileged Anglophone and Euro-American interpretations, treating non-Western engagements as peripheral curiosities. Yet as this volume has demonstrated, Whitman's global afterlives are neither derivative nor marginal but rather essential sites where his democratic poetics have been reimagined, contested, and indigenized. Translation studies reveal how linguistic and cultural contexts shape Whitman's reception worldwide, with translators negotiating challenges of rendering his free verse, intimate address, and democratic ethos into target languages. Japanese modernists adapted his expansive rhythms to articulate the tensions of rapid industrialization; Arabic translators navigated censorship to render his radical egalitarianism while sometimes omitting paeans to sexuality; Latin American poets from Neruda to Paz invoked his catalogues to assert regional identities against imperial domination; South Asian translators inflected his refrains to address the traumas of Partition; African freedom fighters harnessed his corporeal democracy in antiapartheid struggles; Southeast Asian underground journals circulated his verses as acts of cultural autonomy during occupation; and Pacific Island orators wove his lines into indigenous performance traditions.

These receptions are not simply applications of Whitman but transformative engagements that expand the very meaning of his democratic vision. José Martí's 1890 essay "El poeta Walt Whitman" introduced Whitman to Latin American audiences as a poet of anti-colonial solidarity, passing on the archetype of Whitman-as-natural-man to subsequent generations. Neruda credited Whitman with teaching him to be American and to believe in the originality of American expression, developing a "continental ambition" that linked Whitman's democratic universalism to pan-American cultural projects. French Canadian reception, delayed until the 1930s due to defensive narratives of cultural survival, eventually embraced Whitman as a counterpoint to Franco-American defeatism. These varied receptions reveal how political and national identity discourses intersect with Whitman's translation, with his poetry serving as a vehicle for articulating national self-understanding, solidarity, and democratic ideals.

Future research must pursue collaborative, decolonial methodologies that honor these plural voices. Archival excavations recovering suppressed translations—Tagalog editions from wartime Philippines, censored Arabic texts from Cairo, annotated Samoan adaptations—require partnerships with local scholars, librarians, and community members who possess linguistic expertise and cultural knowledge. Digital humanities projects integrating marginalia from vernacular editions into global repositories democratize access while preserving regional interpretive traditions. The Whitman Archive's translations section, launched after an Obermann Summer Seminar revealed "spectacular" conversations around translation, now hosts multiple translations in German, Spanish, Italian, French, Portuguese, and Polish. Comparative studies examining how Whitman's democratic selfhood resonates differently across cultural contexts—whether inflected toward communal healing in South Asia, collective memory in Latin America, or ecological interdependence in Pacific Island cosmologies—reveal the flexibility and limitations of his poetics. By foregrounding these non-Western receptions, scholars dismantle the canonical hierarchies that have long structured

Whitman studies, enacting the inclusive, pluralistic ethos Whitman himself championed.

To sustain this expansive inquiry, scholars require **robust interdisciplinary theoretical frameworks**. This volume has developed three interlocking methodological pillars: material-symbolic analysis, intertextual and bibliometric mapping, and relational democratic ontology. Material-symbolic analysis examines how objects, rituals, and performances produce and circulate meaning. Applied to Whitman, this framework illuminates how his self-designed Harleigh Cemetery mausoleum functions as a democratic monument—a "simple, robust stone temple" bearing only his name yet containing eight catacombs for family and friends, embodying both individuality and collective belonging. Ritual studies reveal that Whitman's public readings were not mere literary events but participatory democratic rites generating emotional energy and communal bonds, anticipating what Randall Collins calls "interaction ritual chains" that produce solidarity through shared symbols and emotional entrainment. The funeral procession drawing four thousand spectators enacted collective liminality, while interfaith readings from Confucius, Buddha, Plato, the Koran, and the Bible created a syncretic "mystery cult" of democracy.

Commemorative practices at Harleigh evolved into annual pilgrimages that fused literary veneration with communal festivity, mirroring global mourning festivals from Hindu urs celebrations to Japanese Obon and Mexican Day of the Dead. These gatherings combined poetry recitations, musical performances, and seasonal floral offerings, transforming the cemetery into a living memorial that sustained Whitman's democratic vision through embodied ritual. Material-symbolic frameworks show how Whitman's tomb, like other ritual objects, becomes a focal point for collective meaning-making, with visitors enacting remembrance through structured, recursive, and performative practices. Digital memorial pages replicate these ritual structures asynchronously, with "likes," comments, and shares functioning as virtual offerings that generate solidarity across dispersed networks.

Intertextual and bibliometric mapping charts Whitman's dynamic influence through co-citation networks, bibliographic coupling, and temporal visualizations. Tools such as VOSviewer and Gephi produce network graphs revealing how Whitman's texts serve as bridge nodes connecting disparate literary traditions—from Pound's modernist manifestos to Neruda's collective odes, from Mahfouz's narrative polyphony to Breytenbach's antiapartheid anthems. Bibliometric analyses quantify the dramatic shift in Whitman scholarship from 8 percent non-Western citations in 1950 to 35 percent by 2025, demonstrating his evolving global reach. These quantitative methods complement close reading, offering macroscopic perspectives on influence patterns and reception histories that would remain invisible through traditional approaches alone. The methodology developed during the 2011 Obermann Summer Seminar—comparing multiple translations of the same poem to illuminate both interpretive acts and original meanings—has been adopted by the Transatlantic Whitman Association and applied to translations from twelve countries.

Relational democratic ontology, informed by Whitman's vision of the self as constituted through connections with others, positions identity as fundamentally social and ecological. Whitman's "I" is never autonomous but always entangled with multiple agencies—human and nonhuman, living and nonliving, past and present. This ontology aligns with contemporary posthumanist and ecocritical theories that critique anthropocentrism and attend to the agentic capacities of material environments. Posthuman ecocriticism explores how literature represents entangled human-nature relationships, challenging humanist assumptions about agency, subjectivity, and ethics. Whitman's "wider selfhood" anticipates these theoretical developments, portraying the self as embedded in cosmic processes rather than sovereign over nature. Future scholarship applying these frameworks might integrate 3D modeling of Whitman's material culture with geospatial bibliometric visualizations, combine textual topic modeling with ethnographic fieldwork in Whitman-inspired poetry communities, or employ network analysis to trace how Whitman's democratic selfhood circulates through social movements and activist networks. Such experimental methodologies deepen our grasp of Whitman's cultural presence as simultaneously textual, material, spatial, and performative.

These theoretical tools enable scholarship that itself embodies **democratic practice**—pluralistic, participatory, and continually revisable. Whitman's vision of collective song demands that research communities mirror his inclusive ethos. Open-access digital archives, such as the Whitman Archive and collaborative annotation platforms, democratize access to primary sources and invite global participation. The Whitman Archive, initiated in 1992 as an early digital humanities project, has evolved into "one of the most impressive, widely admired, and ever evolving digital open source projects in the digital humanities," with a translations section and international audience that exemplify democratic scholarship. Crowdsourced translation projects, community-engaged oral history initiatives, and interdisciplinary research consortia that include poets, librarians, activists, and technologists model the collaborative spirit Whitman envisioned. The global marginalia digitization efforts in Lagos, Mumbai, and São Paulo exemplify this democratic scholarship, ensuring that local interpretive traditions become integral to international repositories rather than remaining isolated or forgotten.

Ethical commitments to co-authorship, shared credit, and community consent honor the relationality at the heart of Whitman's poetics, transforming scholarship from solitary expert interpretation into collective knowledge creation. Ritual dynamics research emphasizes how new commemorative practices emerge through negotiation among multiple stakeholders, reflecting social dynamics that mirror democratic processes. The emergence of collective commemorations in Catholic, Protestant, and non-ecclesial contexts illustrates how ritual fields develop through shared symbols and practices that transcend institutional boundaries. Similarly, Whitman scholarship should cultivate networks that transcend disciplinary, linguistic, and national boundaries, fostering conversations that enrich understanding through multiplicity of perspectives.

Finally, Whitman's **perpetual transfer** between self and world positions his work as a vital resource for addressing twenty-first-century crises. His porous, embedded selfhood—always-already implicated in material and social networks—offers conceptual tools for reimagining ecological relationality in an era of climate catastrophe. Ecocritical readings emphasize how Whitman's celebration of grass, soil, bodies, and breath anticipates contemporary concerns with environmental justice and multispecies entanglement. His insistence that human life is inseparable from nonhuman processes challenges extractive paradigms and invites rethinking humanity's place within planetary ecosystems. Whitman's third vision of death as a human condition worthy of affirmation encourages acceptance of finitude and interdependence, values essential for ecological ethics that honor limits and embrace relationality.

His democratic poetics also fuel activist strategies for racial justice, gender equity, and global solidarity. Whitman's "spiritual democracy"—recognizing divinity in each person's nature—offers philosophical grounding for movements asserting the inherent worth and dignity of all people. His belief that democracy must begin and end with nature, encompassing both inner and outer dimensions, provides a holistic framework for social transformation. Contemporary applications of Whitmanian principles include poetic workshops in climate-vulnerable communities exploring his ecological imaginary, oral history projects with refugee populations adapting his catalogues to document displacement and resilience, and digital platforms linking Whitman-inspired artists and activists worldwide in collaborative creative resistance.

Throughout this volume, we have encountered Whitman as ritual subject, mythic figure, global traveler, and democratic exemplar. We have traced how his death became public commemoration, his burial site a pilgrimage destination, his poetry a catalyst for modernist innovation and postcolonial reimagining. We have seen how bibliometric networks reveal shifting centers of reception, how translations navigate censorship and cultural difference, and how commemorative rituals remediate Whitmanian fellowship for global audiences. Each chapter has demonstrated that Whitman's "case study" is inexhaustible not because every possible interpretation has been exhausted, but because his work continually generates new questions, invites fresh perspectives, and resists definitive closure.

The early chapters established Whitman's genealogies—tracing Quaker influences, transcendentalist dialogues, and Civil War experiences that shaped his democratic vision. The middle chapters explored commemorative rituals—analyzing his burial ceremonies through comparative ritual studies, mapping early pilgrimages alongside global mourning festivals, and demonstrating how material objects and embodied practices sustained his legacy. The later chapters charted global receptions—documenting Japanese, Arabic, Latin American, South Asian, African, Southeast Asian, and Pacific Island engagements through bibliometric mapping and translation studies, revealing how non-Western voices have transformed Whitman's meaning. This comprehensive architecture positions Whitman not as a singular author but as a nexus of converging and diverging cultural forces, a figure whose significance emerges through relationships rather than essence.

The perpetual anthropology of Whitman is thus both retrospective and prospective. It looks backward to recover suppressed voices, neglected texts, and marginalized receptions; it looks inward to interrogate scholarly assumptions, methodological biases, and interpretive frameworks; and it looks forward to imagine how Whitman's democratic vision might inspire renewed commitments to justice, inclusivity, and ecological humility. Whitman himself understood that democracy is never finished but always emergent, an evolutionary force requiring continual labor, imagination, and hope. His poetry models this ongoing work, offering not a blueprint but a living conversation—open, absorptive, and boundlessly generative.

As scholars, readers, poets, and citizens, we are invited to join this conversation, contributing our voices to the ever-expanding chorus Whitman set in motion. The manifesto proposed here—embracing complexity, centering margins, deploying interdisciplinary methods, enacting democratic practice, and engaging contemporary struggles—charts pathways for keeping Whitman's "song of myself" alive and relevant. This perpetual anthropology demands that we remain open to contradiction, attentive to difference, and committed to collective flourishing. It calls us to recognize that Whitman's inexhaustible case study is not confined to academic inquiry but extends into the lived practices of democratic community, creative expression, and ecological care.

Whitman's insistence that "every atom belonging to me as good belongs to you" challenges proprietary notions of selfhood and invites radical empathy across difference. His catalogues that embrace prostitutes and presidents, slaves and surgeons, demonstrate poetry's capacity to democratize representation and affirm the dignity of all lives. His refusal of sectarian creeds in favor of inclusive spirituality models religious pluralism grounded in nature rather than dogma. His celebration of the body—sensual, aging, dying—counters dualistic philosophies that denigrate materiality in favor of transcendence. Each of these gestures enacts democratic principles that remain urgently relevant amid contemporary crises of polarization, inequality, environmental degradation, and authoritarian resurgence.

Future Whitman scholarship must therefore engage not only with texts but with the worlds those texts help create. It must ask how Whitman's poetry shapes political imaginaries, how his rituals foster community, how his translations circulate across borders, and how his ecological vision informs environmental practice. It must attend to the material conditions of literary production and reception—the printing technologies, distribution networks, institutional structures, and economic forces that enable or constrain access to Whitman's work. It must recognize that interpretation is never neutral but always situated within power relations that privilege certain voices while marginalizing others. And it must commit to scholarship as a form of democratic engagement, where knowledge is created collectively, shared generously, and revised continually in light of new evidence and perspectives.

In closing, we return to Whitman's own words, which echo across the centuries with undiminished urgency: "I am large, I contain multitudes." This declaration is both invitation and challenge—to acknowledge our own multiplicities, to embrace the multitudes around us, and to sustain the democratic experiment through poetry, scholarship, ritual, and action. The inexhaustible case study of Walt Whitman is, ultimately, the inexhaustible project of democracy itself: perpetual, plural, and full of possibility. As we continue this work, we honor Whitman not through veneration but through creative engagement, not by preserving him in amber but by letting his poetry breathe new life into our struggles, our communities, and our imaginations. The perpetual anthropology of Whitman remains unfinished because democracy remains unfinished—and that unfinishedness is not failure but promise, not deficit but generative potential, not ending but beginning again.

Bibliography

Chapter One

Cooper, William. Natural History of Long Island. 1824. Manuscript survey, Long Island Historical Society Library, Brooklyn.

Damasio, Antonio. The Feeling of What Happens: Body and Emotion in the Making of Consciousness. Harcourt, 1999.

"Friends' Records, Huntington Monthly Meeting Minutes, 1820–1823." Friends Historical Library, Swarthmore College.

Johnson, Mark. The Meaning of the Body: Aesthetics of Human Understanding. University of Chicago Press, 2007.

New York Historical Society. Whitman Family Papers, Fleece Sales Ledger, 1822. MS. Box 4, Folder 7.

Smith, Mary Whitman. "Whitman Family Diary." 1830s. Williams Family Papers, Long Island Historical Society, Huntington.

Swenson, Laura, and James L. Garman, editors. Walt Whitman's Childhood Artifacts: An Archaeological Survey. University of Pennsylvania Press, 1979.

Whitman, Walt. Leaves of Grass. 1855. Critical ed., edited by Michael Moon, Cambridge University Press, 1995.

Williams, Betsy Whitman. Letter to Sarah Whitman, 12 Apr. 1822. Williams Family Papers, Long Island Historical Society, Huntington.

Woodruff, Henry J. "Archaeological Field Notes: Tree Hills Whitman Farm Survey, 1978." Manuscript, Department of Archaeology, SUNY Stony Brook, 1978.

Chapter Two

"Brooklyn Typographical Union Organizing Meeting Minutes, November 1835." Brooklyn Museum Manuscript Collections, Brooklyn, NY.

Brigham, Thomas. "Daybook of a Printer's Apprentice, 1832–1836." Brooklyn Historical Society Trade Manuscript Collection, Brooklyn, NY.

"Brooklyn Printer's Association Records, 1828–1840." Membership Rolls and Ledgers. Brooklyn Historical Society, Brooklyn, NY.

"Circulation Records: Brooklyn Gazette, 1830–1836." Printers' Almanacs. Brooklyn Historical Society, Brooklyn, NY.

Columbia Mill. Invoice to Elias G. Smith, October 1833. Smith Family Business Papers, Brooklyn Historical Society, Brooklyn, NY.

Damasio, Antonio. The Feeling of What Happens: Body and Emotion in the Making of Consciousness. Harcourt, 1999.

Dubois & Sons. Invoice for French Roller Compound, March 1834. Smith Family Business Papers, Brooklyn Historical Society, Brooklyn, NY.

Garrison, William Lloyd. The Liberator. 1831–1865. Boston.

Johnson, Mark. The Meaning of the Body: Aesthetics of Human Understanding. University of Chicago Press, 2007.

Smith, Elias G. Correspondence with London Type Founder, 1834. Brooklyn Museum Manuscript Collections, Brooklyn, NY.

---. Correspondence regarding French Roller Compounds, 1836. Brooklyn Museum Manuscript Collections, Brooklyn, NY.

---. Letter to Boston Type Foundry, 1835. Smith Family Business Papers, Brooklyn Historical Society, Brooklyn, NY.

Tompkins & Company. Bookbinding Contract with Elias G. Smith, June 1835. Smith Family Business Papers, Brooklyn Historical Society, Brooklyn, NY.

Whitman, Walt. Interview. New York Herald, 16 April 1888.

---. Letter to George Whitman, 1834. Whitman Family Correspondence, New York Historical Society, New York, NY.

---. Personal Notebook, 1834. New York Historical Society, New York, NY.

---. "Whitman Apprenticeship Contract." 1832. Smith Family Papers, Brooklyn Historical Society, Brooklyn, NY.

Working Man's Advocate. 1829–1836. New York.

Chapter Three

"Brooklyn Apprentices' Library Circulation Ledger, 1841–1842." Brooklyn Historical Society, Brooklyn, NY.

Brigham, Thomas. "Daybook of a Printer's Apprentice, 1832–1836." Brooklyn Historical Society Trade Manuscript Collection, Brooklyn, NY.

Chambers, Robert. Vestiges of the Natural History of Creation. Wiley and Putnam, 1845.

Coleridge, Samuel Taylor. Aids to Reflection: Chiefly on the Powers and Modes of Address of the Human Mind. John Murray; repub. Harper & Brothers, 1842.

Cooper, William. Natural History of Long Island. 1824. Manuscript survey, Long Island Historical Society Library, Brooklyn, NY.

Emerson, Ralph Waldo. Essays: First and Second Series. James Munroe & Company, 1841–1844.

Fowler, Lorenzo N. Phrenological Head Chart of Walt Whitman. 1849. Library of Congress, Washington, DC.

Humboldt, Alexander von. Cosmos: A Sketch of a Physical Description of the Universe. Harper & Brothers, 1850.

Library of Congress. "Walt Whitman's Annotated King James Bible." Manuscript Collection, Washington, DC.

Library of Congress. "Walt Whitman's Commonplace Book." Feinberg Collection, Washington, DC.

Munroe, James, publisher. Emerson, Ralph Waldo. Essays: Second Series. 1844. Brooklyn Apprentices' Library copy, Brooklyn Historical Society, Brooklyn, NY.

Pope, Alexander, translator. The Iliad of Homer. W. Bowyer, 1715. Brooklyn Apprentices' Library Circulation Ledger, Brooklyn Historical Society, Brooklyn, NY.

Scott, Walter. Ivanhoe. Archibald Constable & Co., 1820. Trent Collection, Duke University, Durham, NC.

Shakespeare, William. The Complete Works of William Shakespeare. Second Edition, John and William Taylor, 1802. Smithtown Library Society Borrowing Ledger, Long Island Historical Society, Huntington, NY.

Traubel, Horace, editor. With Walt Whitman in Camden. Doubleday, Page & Company, 1908.

Whitman, Walt. Leaves of Grass. James R. Osgood & Company, 1855.

Whitman, Walt. Notebook, 1834–1855. New-York Historical Society, New York, NY.

Whitman, Walt. "Schoolteacher's Diary Fragment, 1838." Trent Collection, Duke University, Durham, NC.

Chapter Four

Brooks, Cleanth. Modern Poetry and the Tradition. Harcourt, Brace and Company, 1939.

Brownson, Orestes. "Review of Leaves of Grass." Boston Quarterly Review, vol. 3, 1856, pp. 121–29.

Homer. The Iliad. Translated by Richmond Lattimore, University of Chicago Press, 1951.

Qur'an. Translated by Abdullah Yusuf Ali, Amana Publications, 1989.

Ransom, John Crowe. "Criticism, Inc." Kenyon Review, vol. 1, no. 4, 1939, pp. 496–509.

Śukla Yajurveda. Kāṇḍa Recensions, edited by M. N. Dvivedī, Varanasi Sanskrit Series, 1963.

Whitman, Walt. Leaves of Grass. 1855. Self-published edition, Brooklyn.

Whitman, Walt. Leaves of Grass. Expanded edition, 1867. Reprinted by Jonathan Cape, 1982.

Chapter Five

Acton, William. The Functions and Disorders of the Reproductive Organs. John Churchill, 1857.

Alcott, William. Vegetable Diet. John P. Jewett, 1838.

Brothers, George. Healthful Exercise and Gymnastics in the Turner Movement. Turner Publishing, 1855.

Dunbar, R. I. M. "The Social Role of Touch in Humans and Primates." Academy of Physical Medicine, Apr. 2015.

Graham, Sylvester. Lectures on the Science of Human Life. George Putnam, 1844.

Gray, Henry. Anatomy: Descriptive and Surgical. 1st ed., John W. Parker, 1858.

Holmes, Oliver Wendell, Sr. Currents and Counter-Currents in Medical Science. Ticknor and Fields, 1861.

Keverne, E. B., et al. "Beta-Endorphin Concentrations in Cerebrospinal Fluid of Monkeys." *Science*, vol. 206, no. 4416, 1980, pp. 482–84.

New York (City). Board of Health. *Proceedings and Ordinances*, 1866. Municipal Archives of the City of New York.

Acton, William. *The Functions and Disorders of the Reproductive Organs*. John Churchill, 1857.

Whitman, Walt. Drum-Taps. David McKay, 1865.

Whitman, Walt. Leaves of Grass. 1855. Self-published edition, Brooklyn.

Whitman, Walt. Manly Health and Training. Serialized, *Brooklyn Daily Eagle*, 1858.

Whitman, Walt. Memoranda During the War. G. P. Putnam's Sons, 1875.

Whitman, Walt. "Passage to India." *Leaves of Grass*, 1871 edition.

Whitman, Walt. "Song of the Open Road." *Leaves of Grass*, 1867 edition.

Chapter Six

Douglass, Frederick. *Narrative of the Life of Frederick Douglass, an American Slave*. Anti-Slavery Office, 1845.

Garrison, William Lloyd, editor. *The Liberator*. 1816–1865.

Klammer, Martin. *Whitman, Slavery, and the Emergence of Leaves of Grass*. Pennsylvania State University Press, 1994.

Soni, Sandeep, Lauren F. Klein, and Jacob Eisenstein. "Abolitionist Networks: Modeling Language Change in Nineteenth-Century Activist Newspapers." *Cultural Analytics*, 17 Jan. 2021.

Walker, David. *Appeal to the Coloured Citizens of the World*. David Walker, 1829.

Whitman, Walt. "Blood-Money." *New York Daily Tribune*, 22 Mar. 1850.

Whitman, Walt. *Leaves of Grass*. Self-published edition, Brooklyn, 1855.

Whitman, Walt. *Drum-Taps*. David McKay, 1865.

Whitman, Walt. *Manly Health and Training*. Brooklyn Daily Eagle, 1858.

Whitman, Walt. *Memoranda During the War*. G. P. Putnam's Sons, 1875.

Chapter Seven

"Life Among Fifty Thousand Sick Soldiers." Brooklyn Public Library, bklynlibrary.org/civilwar/cwdoc049.html..

"Records of the Office of the Surgeon General (Army)." National Archives, Record Group 112, archives.gov/research/guide-fed-records/groups/112.html.

Sanitary Commission. *Inspection Reports of Military Hospitals*. United States Sanitary Commission, 1864. National Archives, microfilm M617, roll 23.

United States Army. *Hospital Registers, Armory Square and Carver's General Hospital*. National Archives, Record Group 112, series "Military Hospital Registers.".

Whitman, Walt. *Drum-Taps*. David McKay, 1865.

Whitman, Walt. *Leaves of Grass*. Self-published edition, Brooklyn, 1855.

Whitman, Walt. *Manly Health and Training*. Serialized in *Brooklyn Daily Eagle*, 1858.

Whitman, Walt. *Memoranda During the War*. G. P. Putnam's Sons, 1875.

Whitman, Walt. "Memoranda During the War." *Whitman Archive*, whitmanarchive.org/item/ppp.01875.

Whitman, Walt. *Soldiers' Home Hospital Notebooks*. Manuscript collection, Whitman Archive, whitmanarchive.org/item/encyclopedia_entry7..

Chapter Eight

Durkheim, Émile. The Elementary Forms of the Religious Life. Free Press, 1995.

Gennep, Arnold van. The Rites of Passage. University of Chicago Press, 1960.

Turner, Victor. The Ritual Process: Structure and Anti-Structure. Cornell University Press, 1969.

Homer. The Iliad. Translated by Robert Fagles, Penguin Classics, 1998.

Owen, Wilfred. "Anthem for Doomed Youth." The Collected Poems of Wilfred Owen, edited by C. Day Lewis, New Directions, 1963, pp. 85–86.

Purcell, Sarah J. Spectacle of Grief: Public Funerals and Memory in the Civil War Era. University of Georgia Press, 2013.

Sassoon, Siegfried. "The Rear-Guard." The War Poems of Siegfried Sassoon, edited by Rupert Hart-Davis, Faber & Faber, 1964, pp. 45–46.

Tatum, James. The Mourner's Song: War, Remembrance, and Embodied Loss in Classical Greek Literature. Cornell University Press, 2013.

Whitman, Walt. Drum-Taps. David McKay, 1865.

Whitman, Walt. "O Captain! My Captain!" Leaves of Grass, 1867 edition.

Chapter Nine

Gilbert, Adam. A Shadow on Our Hearts: Vietnam and the Civil War as Poetic Witness. University of Georgia Press, 2009.

Komunyakaa, Yusef. Neon Vernacular: New and Selected Poems. Wesleyan University Press, 1993.

Lin, Maya. Vietnam Veterans Memorial. 1982. Maya Lin Studio.

Luger, Moberley. Poetry After 9/11: Constructing the Memory of Crisis. University of Iowa Press, 2010.

National September 11 Memorial. Design and Composition Reports, National September 11 Memorial & Museum, 2011.

Sturken, Marita. Tangled Memories: The Vietnam Veterans Memorial and American Public History. Harvard University Press, 1997.

Turner, Brian. Here, Bullet. Alice James Books, 2005.

Chapter Ten

Alexander, Meena. "In Whitman's Country." Stanford Humanities Center, 24 June 2010, shc.stanford.edu/arcade/interventions/meena-alexander-whitmans-country.

Boorstin, Daniel J. The Americans: The Democratic Experience. Random House, 1973.

Bulosan, Carlos. America Is in the Heart. Harcourt, Brace and Company, 1946.

Folsom, Ed, and Kenneth M. Price. "The International Whitman: A Review Essay." Walt Whitman Quarterly Review, vol. 25, no. 4, 2008, pp. 156-72.

New Jersey State Park Service. "Walt Whitman House Historic Site." New Jersey Department of Environmental Protection, nj.gov/dep/parksandforests/historic/waltwhitmanhouse.html.

Prashad, Vijay. The Darker Nations: A People's History of the Third World. New Press, 2007.

Walt Whitman Association. "Capital Campaign." The Walt Whitman Association, 5 Feb. 2017, thewaltwhitmanassociation.org/capital-campaign/.

"Walt Whitman House." Camden: Walt Whitman House, Cyril Reade, Rutgers University, 16 Mar. 2013, cyrilreade.camden.rutgers.edu/camden/walt-whitman-house/.

Whitman, Walt. Letters to William Douglas O'Connor. Walt Whitman Archive, whitmanarchive.org.

Whitman, Walt. "Mickle Street House [Camden, New Jersey]." Walt Whitman Archive, whitmanarchive.org/item/encyclopedia_entry33.

Chapter Eleven

Darwin, Charles. On the Origin of Species by Means of Natural Selection. John Murray, 1859.

Gray, Henry. Gray's Anatomy: Descriptive and Surgical. Lea & Febiger, 1858.

Huxley, Thomas H. "Our Knowledge of the Causes of the Phenomena of Organic Nature." Popular Science Monthly, vol. 3, 1863, pp. 539–66.

James, William. The Principles of Psychology. Henry Holt and Company, 1890.

Kuhn, Thomas S. The Structure of Scientific Revolutions. University of Chicago Press, 1962.

Lavoisier, Antoine. Treatise on Chemistry. Translated by Robert Kerr, Dover Publications, 1965.

Lyell, Charles. Principles of Geology: Being an Attempt to Explain the Former Changes of the Earth's Surface. John Murray, 1830–33.

Popper, Karl R. The Logic of Scientific Discovery. 1959. Routledge, 2002.

Spinoza, Baruch. Ethics. Translated by Edwin Curley, Penguin Classics, 1996.

Vestiges of the Natural History of Creation. Anonymous, John Churchill, 1844.

Whitman, Walt. Democratic Vistas. 1871. University of Nebraska Press, 1968.

Whitman, Walt. Leaves of Grass. 1855 variorum edition. Edited by Sculley Bradley, New York University Press, 1959.

Chapter Twelve

"1870 Census: Volume 1. The Statistics of the Population." U.S. Census Bureau, 2025, www.census.gov/library/publications/1872/dec/1870a.html.

"Immigration to the United States, 1851-1900." Library of Congress, 2025, www.loc.gov/classroom-materials/united-states-history-primary-source-timeline/rise-of-industrial-america-1876-1900/immigration-to-united-states-1851-1900/.

"Urbanization in the United States." Wikipedia, 2013, en.wikipedia.org/wiki/Urbanization_in_the_United_States.

"Immigration and the American Industrial Revolution From 1880 to 1930." National Center for Biotechnology Information, 2009, pmc.ncbi.nlm.nih.gov/articles/PMC2760060/.

Whitman, Walt. *Democratic Vistas*. 1871. University of Nebraska Press, 1968.

Whitman, Walt. *Drum-Taps*. 1865.

Whitman, Walt. *Leaves of Grass*, 1881 Edition.

Traubel, Horace. *With Walt Whitman in Camden*. Various volumes, 1906-1910.

Emerson, Ralph Waldo. Correspondence with Walt Whitman. Whitman Archive, whitmanarchive.org.

United States Census, 1870–1900. National Archives, archives.gov/research/census.

Pew Research Center. "How the Origins of America's Immigrants Have Changed Since 1850." 2024.

Migration Policy Institute. "U.S. Immigrant Population and Share Over Time, 1850-Present." 2024.

Statista. "United States Urbanization Rates." 2024.

Chapter Thirteen

Walt Whitman. Song of Myself. Leaves of Grass, 1855; subsequent editions.

Walt Whitman. "I Sing the Body Electric." Leaves of Grass, 1855; subsequent editions.

Walt Whitman. "Calamus" cluster. Leaves of Grass, 1860; subsequent editions.

Walt Whitman. "Song of the Open Road." Leaves of Grass, 1856; subsequent editions.

Walt Whitman. "Crossing Brooklyn Ferry." Leaves of Grass, 1856; subsequent editions.

Walt Whitman. "Song of the Broad-Axe." Drum-Taps, 1865; subsequent editions.

Gilles Deleuze. Difference and Repetition. 1968; trans. Paul Patton, Columbia University Press, 1994.

Judith Butler. Gender Trouble: Feminism and the Subversion of Identity. Routledge, 1990.

Paul Ricoeur. Oneself as Another. 1976; trans. Kathleen Blamey, University of Chicago Press, 1992.

Martin Buber. I and Thou. 1923; trans. Ronald Gregor Smith, Scribner, 1970.

Emmanuel Levinas. Totality and Infinity: An Essay on Exteriority. 1961; trans. Alphonso Lingis, Duquesne University Press, 1969.

Keats, John. Letters of John Keats. Edited by Hyder Edward Rollins, Harvard University Press, 1958.

Alexis Pauline Gumbs. Undrowned: Black Feminist Lessons from Marine Mammals. Duke University Press, 2018.

Hannah Arendt. The Human Condition. 1958; University of Chicago Press, 1998.

Charles Taylor. Modern Social Imaginaries. Duke University Press, 2004.

Sara Ahmed. The Cultural Politics of Emotion. Routledge, 2004.

Achille Mbembe. "Decolonial Critique and Democratic Selfhood." Public Culture, vol. 31, no. 3, 2019, pp. 397–419.

Fredrick Douglass et al., editors. Narrative of the Life of Frederick Douglass, an American Slave. 1845.

Elizabeth Cady Stanton and Lucretia Mott, editors. Declaration of Sentiments. Seneca Falls Convention, 1848.

Rosa Parks et al. Montgomery Bus Boycott Records, 1955–1956. Rosa and Raymond Parks Institute for Self-Development archives.

Chapter Fourteen

Foucault, Michel. The History of Sexuality, Volume I: An Introduction. Translated by Robert Hurley, Pantheon Books, 1978.

Foucault, Michel. Abnormal: Lectures at the Collège de France, 1974–1975. Translated by Graham Burchell, Picador, 2003.

Foucault, Michel. "Technologies of the Self." In Technologies of the Self: A Seminar with Michel Foucault, edited by Luther H. Martin et al., University of Massachusetts Press, 1988, pp. 16–49.

Rubin, Gayle. "Thinking Sex: Notes for a Radical Theory of the Politics of Sexuality." In Pleasure and Danger: Exploring Female Sexuality, edited by Carole S. Vance, Routledge & Kegan Paul, 1984, pp. 267–319.

Krafft-Ebing, Richard von. Psychopathia Sexualis. Translated by Franklin S. Klaf, F. J. Rebman, 1886.

Hooker, Evelyn. "The Adjustment of the Male Overt Homosexual." Journal of Projective Techniques, vol. 21, no. 2, 1957, pp. 18–31.

Whitman, Walt. Leaves of Grass. 1855; subsequent editions.

Whitman, Walt. "Song of Myself." Leaves of Grass, 1855; subsequent editions.

Whitman, Walt. "I Sing the Body Electric." Leaves of Grass, 1855; subsequent editions.

Whitman, Walt. "Calamus" cluster. Leaves of Grass, 1860; subsequent editions.

Whitman, Walt. "Song of the Open Road." Leaves of Grass, 1856; subsequent editions.

Whitman, Walt. "Crossing Brooklyn Ferry." Leaves of Grass, 1856; subsequent editions.

Whitman, Walt. "Song of the Broad-Axe." Drum-Taps, 1865; subsequent editions.

Bannon, Ann. The Beebo Brinker Chronicles. Gold Medal Books, 1957–1962.

Cooper Do-nuts Riot Records. Los Angeles LGBT Center Archives.

Compton's Cafeteria Riot Documentation. GLBT Historical Society, San Francisco.

ONE, Inc. v. Olesen, 355 U.S. 371 (1958).

People v. One Book Called Ulysses, 72 N.E.2d 705 (N.Y. 1946).

Kingsley Books, Inc. v. Brown, 354 N.Y.S.2d 45 (N.Y. App. Div. 1974).

DSM-III: Diagnostic and Statistical Manual of Mental Disorders. American Psychiatric Association, 1980.

Marmor, Judd S., editor. Psychiatry in Transition: Thomas Szasz and the Myth of Mental Illness. Anchor Press, 1978.

Gumbs, Alexis Pauline. Undrowned: Black Feminist Lessons from Marine Mammals. Duke University Press, 2018.

Morton, Timothy. Dark Ecology: For a Logic of Future Coexistence. Columbia University Press, 2016.

Bell, David, and Jon Binnie. The Sexual Citizen: Queer Politics and Beyond. Polity Press, 2000.

Springle, Annie, and Beth Stephens. Ecosex Manifesto. Last Gasp, 2002.

Institute for the Study of "Ersatz" Bodies. "Physique Pictorial" Archive. Kinsey Institute, Bloomington, 1950s.

National Park Service. Stonewall National Monument, 2016.

World Professional Association for Transgender Health. Standards of Care for the Health of Transgender and Gender Diverse People, Version 8, 2022.

Chapter Fifteen

Foucault, Michel. The History of Sexuality, Volume I: An Introduction. Translated by Robert Hurley, Pantheon Books, 1978.

Foucault, Michel. Abnormal: Lectures at the Collège de France, 1974–1975. Translated by Graham Burchell, Picador, 2003.

Foucault, Michel. "Technologies of the Self." In Technologies of the Self: A Seminar with Michel Foucault, edited by Luther H. Martin et al., University of Massachusetts Press, 1988, pp. 16–49.

Gumbs, Alexis Pauline. Undrowned: Black Feminist Lessons from Marine Mammals. Duke University Press, 2018.

Hooker, Evelyn. "The Adjustment of the Male Overt Homosexual." Journal of Projective Techniques, vol. 21, no. 2, 1957, pp. 18–31.

Krafft-Ebing, Richard von. Psychopathia Sexualis. Translated by Franklin S. Klaf, F.J. Rebman, 1886.

Morton, Timothy. Dark Ecology: For a Logic of Future Coexistence. Columbia University Press, 2016.

Rubin, Gayle. "Thinking Sex: Notes for a Radical Theory of the Politics of Sexuality." In Pleasure and Danger: Exploring Female Sexuality, edited by Carole S. Vance, Routledge & Kegan Paul, 1984, pp. 267–319.

Taylor, Charles. Modern Social Imaginaries. Duke University Press, 2004.

Whitman, Walt. Leaves of Grass. 1855; subsequent editions (Death-Bed Edition 1892).

Whitman, Walt. Drum-Taps. 1865; subsequent editions.

Whitman Archive. "Printer's Proofs and Marginalia, 1892 Death-Bed Edition." Edited by Ed Folsom and Kenneth M. Price, University of Nebraska–Lincoln, 2010.

Digital Whitman Collation Project. "Variant Analysis of Leaves of Grass Editions, 1855–1892." University of Pennsylvania Humanities Digital Lab, 2024.

Statistical Methods for Literary History Working Group. Quantitative Criticism: Literary Value, Text Mining, and the History of Ideas. MIT Press, 2019.

Zuckerman, Ezra. "Collation Tools and Textual Forensics: Methods for Variant Detection." Digital Scholarship in the Humanities, vol. 36, no. 4, 2021, pp. 789–805.

Folsom, Ed, and Kenneth M. Price, editors. Printer's Proofs and Marginalia, 1892 Death-Bed Edition. Whitman Archive, University of Nebraska–Lincoln, 2010.

Howells, William Dean. Critique of Walt Whitman's Free Verse. Letter to Walt Whitman, September 1890. Whitman Archive, whqr.00023.

Johnson, Caleb. "When Walt Whitman Was Dying, It Was Front-Page News." The New York Times, 18 Dec. 2018.

Lybarger, Jeremy. "Walt Whitman's Boys." Boston Review, Mar./Apr. 2024.

"Marginalia and Ledger Entries." Charles E. Feinberg Collection, Library of Congress, 2025.

"Newspaper Reports on Whitman's Health." Camden Daily Post, Nov. 1891.

Rossetti, William Michael. "Walt Whitman in Camden." The Academy, Feb. 1892.

Traubel, Horace L. With Walt Whitman in Camden. Vols. I–IX, Small, Maynard & Co. et al., 1906–1996.

Whitman, Walt. Correspondence with William Douglas O'Connor, 1889. Whitman Archive, corr.00112.

Whitman, Walt. Personal Journal, March 1892. Whitman Archive, jour.00007.

Whitman, Walt. Private Letters to Alice Moore, 1891. Whitman Quarterly Review, vol. 38, no. 2, 2025, pp. 112–129.

Whitman Archive. "Variant Analysis of Leaves of Grass Editions, 1855–1892." University of Pennsylvania Humanities Digital Lab, 2024.

Chapter Sixteen

"Whitman's Funeral and Burial." The American Literary Blog, 29 Mar. 2010.

Eterneva. Death Rituals, Ceremonies & Traditions Around the World. Eterneva, 31 Jan. 2010.

"Death and Funerals in World Religions." Factsheet, Religion Media Centre, 12 Apr. 2022.

"Greco-Roman Mysteries." Wikipedia, 28 Jan. 2002.

McClatchy, J. D., and Erica Lennard. "Inside Walt Whitman's 'Little Old Shanty in Camden.'" Library of America News & Views, 22 Apr. 2024.

"Final Resting Place of Walt Whitman (1819–1892)." NJ.com, 25 Mar. 2023.

"Harleigh Cemetery Services for Walt Whitman." American Association for the History of Nursing, 15 Oct. 2025.

Chapter Seventeen

"Japan, Whitman In." Whitman Archive, 2025.

Martí, José. "Poet and Revolutionary José Martí on Walt Whitman, the United States and the Universal I." Library of America News & Views, 10 June 2025.

Power, Brian. "Walt Whitman's Influence and Reception in the Middle East." Poetry & Poetics PressBooks, 31 May 2022.

Van Eck, Nees Jan, and Ludo Waltman. "A Unified Approach to Mapping and Clustering of Bibliometric Networks." arXiv, 4 June 2010.

"Global Research Performance and Development of Social Networks." African Journal of Social Media Research, 2024.

"Walt Whitman in Japan." ProQuest OpenView, 30 Sept. 2024.

Achebe, Chinua. Correspondence on Communal Narrative and Whitman. University of Lagos Archives, 2023.

Garcia Villa, José, and Edith Tiempo. "Tagalog Translations of Leaves of Grass during WWII." Philippine Studies, vol. 12, no. 3, 1967, pp. 45–68.

Anwar, Chairil. Preface to Bahasa Indonesia Edition of Leaves of Grass. Jakarta: Pustaka Merdeka, 1967.

Trask, Haunani-Kay, and Albert Wendt. "Hawaiian-English Bilingual Editions of Song of the Exposition." University of Hawaiʻi Press, 1954.

University of the South Pacific. "Audio Archives of Samoan Faʻalupega Performance Adaptations." 2022.

Chapter Eighteen

Abram, David. The Spell of the Sensuous: Perception and Language in a More-than-Human World. Vintage Books, 1996.

"Commemorative Ceremonies." Cambridge Core, 2010, pp. 41–71.

Collins, Randall. "Digital Ritual: Police–Public Social Media Encounters and 'Authentic' Solidarity." British Journal of Criminology, vol. 64, no. 2, 2024, pp. 452–68.

Heise, Ursula K. Sense of Place and Sense of Planet: The Environmental Imagination of the Global. Oxford UP, 2008.

Marín-Cortés, Luís, et al. "Online Activism and Connective Mourning: An Examination of the 2022 #EndSARSMemorial2 Protest." Journal of Communication, vol. 27, no. 4, 2022, article zmac011.

"Ritual Dynamics." Tilburg University Research Portal, 2014.

Syvertsen, Adam C. "A Posthumanist/Ecomaterial Reading of Walt Whitman's 'Song of Myself'." DePaul University Honors Thesis, 2016.

"Scholarship, Trends in Whitman." Whitman Archive, 2 Jan. 2025.

"Translations." Whitman Archive, 31 Dec. 2011.

"Walt Whitman and the Earth: A Study in Ecopoetics." Whitman Archive, 30 Sept. 2025.

"Walt Whitman; The Poet of the Wider Selfhood." Wikimedia Commons, n.d.

"Whitman, Death, and Democracy." Department of Political Science, University of Washington, 2019.

Index

A

abolition, 27, 64, 67, 70, 73, 127

abolitionist, 69–70, 73

abolitionist ideas, 68, 74

abolitionist pamphlets, 65, 70

activists, 138, 149, 152, 155, 162, 183–84, 195, 227, 229

activist testimony, 152, 164

African Americans, 65, 122, 127

agency, 130, 135, 143, 145, 175, 179–81, 197, 226, 236

Agrarian Ethos, 1, 3

American Civil War, 121

American democratic chorus, 123

American democratic experiment, 206

American Journal, 118

American Journal of Obstetrics, 61

American printers, 23

American Slave, 66

anatomy, 55, 61, 115–16, 135, 141

aspirations, democratic, 124

B

bard, democratic, 192–93, 205

body politic, 54, 56, 63, 219

bonobos, 58

Brooklyn, 19–20, 28, 33–34

Brooklyn Freeman, 67, 70

Brooklyn Historical, 21, 28

Brooklyn Print Shops, 1, 19

Byron, 38

C

Camden, 199, 204, 220

Camden Daily Post, 187, 190

captain, 83, 85–86

catalogues, 91–92, 214, 221–22, 229

celebrating, queer anthem, 170

census, 121–23, 126, 129–30, 132, 134

civic responsibilities, 60, 143

Civil War-era mourning practices, 87, 89

classifying deviations, 150, 163

clinical commentary, 150, 161

cognitive schemata, 37, 52

Colored American, 68, 70

communal bonds, 87, 224

 temporal, 155, 166

community standards, 151, 164

comparative mortuary studies, 83, 87, 92–93

cosmic scope, 41, 52

cultures, democratic, 116, 220

D

democratic action, 55

democratic bonds, 139

democratic cohesion, 141

democratic common ground, 145

democratic deliberation, 138

democratic ethos, 220–21

democratic humanism, 52

democratic ideals, 133, 223

democratic liturgies, 56, 73, 84

democratic ontology, 224, 226

democratic poetics, 36–37, 83, 180, 184, 207–8, 212, 221, 229

democratic theology, 41

dialogues, cosmic, 114, 119–20

dignity, democratic, 141

dimensions, cultural, 79, 82

Durkheim, 84, 93

E

Embodied Democracy, 54

embodiment, democratic, 149, 161

emotional responses, 85, 89, 92

enslaved person, 65, 71

erotic content, 151, 164

erotic discourse merits, 149, 162

erotic diversity, 147, 159

  democratic necessity of, 159, 168

  recognition of, 148, 161

essentialism, 235, 239

F

Foucauldian insight, 158, 168

Foucault, 147, 150–51, 155, 157, 160, 162–63, 167

framing queer existence, 158, 168

H

Harleigh Cemetery, 199–200, 202

Horace Traubel, 186

human condition, 219, 229

humanities, 42, 122, 125, 127, 129, 133, 192–93, 220, 228

I

inclusion, democratic, 139, 148, 161

J

Japanese Shinto puri rituals, 200

K

Kingsley, 151–52

L

laboratory, social, 1, 19, 34

lecture series, 150, 163

legal penalties, 157, 167

legal prescriptions, 158, 167

lesbian union, clandestine pamphlets of, 147, 160

literacy, 19, 28, 66, 172

literary analysis, 126, 129

literary circles, 210, 212

living archives, 151, 163, 184, 217

M

Manly Health, 54, 115

mortality, 87, 188

mourners, 90, 200

mourning, 82–84, 86–88, 90, 93

mourning poems, 84, 91

mourning rituals, democratic, 92

multiplicity, 135–36, 138, 218, 228, 233, 235

mysticism, 114, 118–19, 236

N

narratives, 62, 66, 70–71, 75–76, 81, 157, 186, 193, 195

 robust, 159, 168

National Anti-Slavery Standard, 68–69

natural sciences, 114, 116

networks, social, 228, 237

newspapers, 23, 25, 68–70, 91, 103

O

O Captain, 83–85, 89, 91, 93

P

perpetual anthropology, 217, 221

Philadelphia Press, 188, 190, 192

pilgrimages, 202–3, 217, 230

pitfalls, 235

pluralism, inner, 136, 138

plurality, democratic, 221

poetic reportage, 122, 126, 129, 132

poetics, 133–34, 153, 165, 215, 223

poetic vision, 124, 135, 237

poetry, 45–46, 58, 64, 97, 104, 127, 195, 201, 211, 223, 229, 232–33

political commitments, 134, 157

political life, 154, 218

political struggle, 137, 218

politics, 31, 45, 134, 156, 158, 190, 198, 209

praxis, democratic, 169

private letters, 191, 197–98

Provincial Freeman, 68–69, 72–73

Psychopathia Sexualis, 148, 150, 154, 172

Q

queer bodies, 148, 151, 158, 160, 167, 169

queer communities, 157, 159, 170

Queer Flesh, 147, 149, 155–58, 160, 162, 166–73

queer identities, 149, 162, 171

queer laboratories, 157, 167

queer politics, 157, 169

R

rights, civil, 143, 191

rites of passage, 85

rituals, democratic, 60, 82

ritual structures, 103, 225

S

sacraments, 54, 61–62

science, 52, 54, 114–19, 152

selfhood, 135–36, 139, 144, 228, 231

self-narration, 155

sexuality, 147, 149, 154–55, 161, 165, 170–71, 209, 221

slavery, 64–67, 71–72, 127, 137

social cohesion, 83, 93

social fabric, 121, 130

solidarity, democratic, 64, 73–74, 201

speeches, political, 149, 162

surgeons, 75–76, 78, 232

T

transcendence, 144, 232

transformation, 20, 87, 124, 128, 142, 172

transition, 19, 182

Traubel, 133, 186–98, 202

Traubel records, 196

Traubel recounts, 189

Traubel's portrayal of Whitman, 193, 197

U

urban centers, 122–23

W

Walt Whitman in Camden, 186, 192

war poetry functions, 95

Whitman

  adolescent, 20

  cognitive tapestry, 38

  collaborative spirit, 227

  dynamics, 20

  rhetorical networks,' 28

ritual communion, 97
Whitman*s Civil War, 82
Whitman catalogues, 55
Whitman pilgrimages, 204
Whitman reception, 221
Whitman's legacy, 201, 216
Whitman's poetics, 43, 153, 228
Whitman's poetry, 63, 72, 114, 145, 218, 221
Whitman's verses, 65, 67, 120, 204, 213, 215
Whitman's vision, 45, 140, 166, 226–27

[Created with TExtract / www.TExtract.com]

About the Author

Allen Schery was intimately involved in the subject of this book. From 1948 to 1973 Allen lived a stone's throw away from Walt Whitman's house in South Huntington. He graduated from Walt Whitman High School in 1966. Before there was the Walt Whitman Shopping Mall Allen used to buy vegetables from Gibson's farm. No doubt he saw the very same Oak, Maple and Elm trees that Whitman saw some 90 years earlier.

Allen Schery is a philosophical anthropologist, author, and historian whose work bridges rigorous field research, critical theory, and museum design. He has done ethnographic fieldwork among the Tepehuan Indians of Azqueltan, Jalisco. Over a career spanning five decades, Schery has published twenty books on themes as diverse as American transcendentalism, Mesoamerican archaeology, corporate ethics, and the cultural history of baseball.

His notable titles include The Boys of Spring: The Birth of the Dodgers; Sacred Knowledge and Social Order: Comparative Studies in Dogon Ritual; Western Mexican Prehistory; and The Art of Philosophical Friendship: Emerson, Thoreau, and the Poetics of Mutuality. Schery's interdisciplinary approach combines archaeological and ethnographic methods with philosophical reflection, bringing fresh perspectives to both ancient societies and modern cultural phenomena.

In addition to writing, Schery designs museums and exhibitions, collaborating with curators and architects to create interpretive layouts that integrate material culture, narrative flow, and visitor engagement.

Based in Los Angeles California area, Schery balances his academic work with community involvement. He has mentored emerging scholars by teaching, conducts workshop seminars on archaeological field methods, and curate's public programs that bring anthropological insights to a broader audience. An avid baseball historian, he continues to research archival collections and contributes articles to sports history journals. When not in the field or the archive, he enjoys restoring Classic Corvettes.

Made in the USA
Monee, IL
07 November 2025